INTAGLIOS
AND RINGS

INTAGLIOS AND RINGS

Greek, Etruscan and Eastern

FROM A PRIVATE COLLECTION

JOHN BOARDMAN

THAMES AND HUDSON · LONDON

Blocks by Gilchrist Brothers Ltd, Leeds
Printed by Alden & Mowbray Ltd at the Alden Press, Oxford
Bound by Mansell (Bookbinders) Ltd, Witham

Contents

IN MEMORIAM
GISELA RICHTER

Preface

The selection of engraved gems presented here is from a large collection which has been formed over the last fifty years. Some are from well-known old cabinets, such as the Southesk, others from more recently formed minor collections – as that of Ephraim (Lugano), the Abbé Nayem (Beirut), and an unidentified German collector whose stones were sold in New York. The rest are the results of purchases in various parts of Europe, from London to Istanbul, the majority being from Italy. The assured South Italian or Sicilian source of many rings and green jasper scarabs acquired from an old collection proves an indication of some importance for determining their place of manufacture. Some nine out of ten of all the pieces published here have never been illustrated before.

A large part of the collection is devoted to Eastern cylinder seals and to Roman intaglios. These have been ignored for the purposes of the present volume, with only sample pieces shown, so that fuller justice could be done to the fine range of Greek and Etruscan stones which are the core of the collection. But here, too, it has proved necessary to be selective. The result is a choice of some two hundred pieces, which illustrate the full range of Greek glyptic from the Late Bronze Age to the Hellenistic, particularly rich in Archaic stones which include two master-pieces assignable to leading artists – the Master of the London Satyr and Epimenes. The finger rings are valuable for the range of silver specimens of Sicilian origin, and a number of Classical gold rings, probably from South Italy. The Greco-Persian series is unusually rich and includes several unique figure and animal studies, while the 'Greco-Phoenician' scarabs fill an important gap in our knowledge of the class, since they are probably from Sicily (Motya), hitherto a poor source for these stones.

The Etruscan series is the most numerous, including a new masterpiece by the Master of the Boston Dionysos. A generous selection of later Etruscan scarabs is presented to demonstrate the variety of styles and subjects. The few Near Eastern stones appended are, as explained, tokens only.

The stones are illustrated by enlarged photographs of the originals, supplemented or replaced by photographs of plaster impressions wherever this seemed desirable, to show details of quality more clearly. For all the visual attractions of photographs of originals, they can often prove defective or misleading in recording style, and for most of the stones shown here the artists' intention was to make a seal which would produce an impression to be admired or to be used to identify property, rather than, or as well as, a jewel to be admired in its own right or in its golden setting. Several of the original settings are preserved with these stones, some of them important testimony to the way in which they were worn or used in antiquity. The study of these settings has been largely neglected by students of both intaglios and jewellery. The photographs are enlarged to varying degrees according to the importance or detail of the cutting.

The photographs of the stones are by the author. Plaster impressions were prepared from the author's impressions or casts by Miss O. Rennie and photographed by the author and by Robert L. Wilkins, to whom warm thanks are also due for careful processing of all prints.

The text itself is intended to provide a narrative on the main classes presented, and further discussion of the iconography or other significance of individual pieces. The Catalogue gives more detailed descriptions and references.

The owner of this collection, to whose acumen this book is a tribute, wishes to remain anonymous. My thanks to him for his kindness in allowing me to study his gems, for his hospitality, and for his decision to make this selection known through a publication, cannot be expressed explicitly, but they are none the less heartfelt.

December, 1973   J.B.

CHAPTER I

Greek Gems

The sealing of property, or the identification of an individual by a blazon or a device such as might appear on a signet ring, is an indication of a degree of social and economic organization attained in antiquity only by the countries of the middle and eastern Mediterranean, and of the older valley civilizations of Egypt and the Near East, before Rome spread the practice to beyond the borders of its empire. In Greece the record was not a continuous one, and the seals of the Bronze Age, which depend on Minoan art, are in a vigorously independent style (*4, 5*). After the palace bureaucracies of Bronze Age Greece had been overthrown or abandoned the country lacked the organization and wealth which called for the practice of sealing, and the arts of cutting seals and gems disappeared. They are found again as Greece recovers close contact with the East, and the seals of the new Geometric age are angular, or simple discs and half spheres, cut roughly in soft stone or ivory, their devices derived from the East or from contemporary styles in other arts. One unusual phenomenon of the seventh and sixth centuries BC was the Island Gems, generally cut in a soft, translucent green serpentine, and imitating the shapes and rarely the motifs of Bronze Age gems found fortuitously, admired and copied by island artists. But the island studios did not confine their activity to the production of these throw-backs. In the same distinctive stone they cut seals of the Geometric forms current in Greece elsewhere, and then, in the later sixth century, a very few artists of merit used the material for the new scarab shape and offer the last essays in Greece of the old hand-cutting techniques for gems. Both of these small but well defined classes are represented in this collection. *6* shows the rough-cut style on an angular, tabloid stone, deceptively primitive unless this is the earliest Greek representation of a folding stool, since this Eastern furniture is not represented on other Greek works before the sixth century. The scarab *2* presents an accomplished study of a lion, more ruggedly conceived in this old hand-cutting technique than the drilled devices of contemporary wheel-cut scarabs (as our *9 – 11*). The shape of the scarab back, which is very roughly sketched, and the modelling of the lion's body suggest that this may be attributed to the artist Onesimos, who signed three surviving scarabs. With other attributions this brings the total of his identified works to nine.

The scarab shape had been introduced to Greek artists before the middle of the sixth century, possibly in Cyprus, and with it the techniques, long forgotten by Greeks, of working hard stone with drill and cutting wheel. The favoured material is cornelian, the favourite subjects a fairly narrow range of animals and human figures from the contemporary Archaic repertory, with occasional admissions of eastern or Phoenician detail. There is a good range of styles in this collection, including two masterpieces, attributable to two of the masters of Archaic Greek glyptic.

7 is a good introduction to the series since it displays most clearly the Eastern aspects of sixth-century gem cutting. The Egyptian god Bes is fighting a lion. Bes was adopted into Phoenician art (compare our *110*), and in works such as this, where his Egyptian origins have been forgotten and we may suspect either a Greek hand or a studio serving either Greeks or Cypriots, he performs as an eastern hero (compare our *85*) or even a Herakles. His feather crown is reduced, and he wears a horse-tail like a Greek satyr. There was commonly confusion between Bes wearing a lion-skin whose tail often falls behind him, and the satyr, and here the tail is decidedly satyric. The lion resembles many of the Greek Common Style but would not be out of place farther east. The fine gold setting – a collar decorated with granulation and twisted gold wire on a swivel hoop – is of a type met in Phoenicia, and in the Punic west, and between these extremes in both Cyprus and Greece. A replica of the whole piece, published only in a poor drawing, was found at Ialysos in Rhodes in a grave with vases of about 520–510 BC, otherwise we could not be sure to which end of the Mediterranean we should attribute this piece.

The following stones have more purely Greek subjects. The gorgoneia on *3* and *8* are an interesting contrast. The monstrous head appears often on Archaic scarabs, rarely on other gems or rings (see our *82*). *8* belongs to a well known group, closely related to the earliest Greek scarabs. *3* follows the same scheme for parts of the head but is quite differently composed on the stone, and the broad grimace with tusks and hanging tongue is reduced to a harmless smirk. The stone may have been found in South Italy, but is not necessarily South Italian work, although it is easy to underestimate the part played by the Greek colonies in South Italy in the gem engraving of this period, and grotesque heads, without the gorgon snakes, appear on later Italian gems, especially in Etruria. Of the monsters, *10* presents an interesting contrast with later griffins (as *100*), the sphinx *9* is commonplace, but the siren standing over or carrying a body (*14*) is worth a moment's attention, not for its style but for its subject. Sphinxes carrying youths are popular subjects on Archaic scarabs, and they may be the Theban sphinx with her victims before Oidipus came to confound her, rather than any death-demon. The siren is more easy to accept as an agent of the other world; there is another gem of this subject of these years, and the best known and most explicit representation appears in the general cultural area to which most Archaic Greek scarabs belong – that of East Greece – on the Harpy Tomb at Xanthos (its sculptures in the British Museum).

1 is a fine work by an anonymous artist we know as the Master of the London Satyr. He likes large scarabs, with careful and distinctively detailed backs, just like this. His name-piece (our *Fig. 6*) is a *tour de force* of composition and effective patterning with the drill, but his other works, with human or animal subjects, are more in keeping with the current styles, less aggressive, and with them goes this new stone. The sinewy legs and belly markings at least recall the name-piece, but the body is less massively conceived, the ears large but not pointed, the feet human, not equine. The kneeling pose is a favourite one for artists who aim to fill the oval field, and the subject – satyr with cup and jug – a popular one. The general style and detailing of the scarab foreshadow Etruscan work, and it has been possible to speculate whether the Master was not an emigrant artist, working in Etruria: but this piece was once in Corinth, which at least suggests a Greek homeland studio, though hardly a Corinthian one. This is the tenth stone attributable to this artist, who worked in the mid-second half of the sixth century. *13* gives a measure of how summarily a similar subject could be treated in other Greek workshops.

The other figure subjects on these Archaic gems, with one notable exception, are less ambitious. There are some good late Archaic Athenas on gems. The one on *12* is remarkable mainly for the simplicity of her dress – chiton alone, with helmet and spear, no aegis or shield – but this simpler Athena type, with spear at ease, has a long history in East Greece. The flying Eros (*15*), cavalier (*11*), boy with lyre (*16*) and Herakles (*17*), are also popular subjects of the later sixth century, the last two presenting the kneeling pose again. With the end of the century this rather primitive posture is abandoned for more upright, but stooping poses, which help dictate new themes – petting a dog, picking up athletic equipment or armour (*19*), greaving, fastening a sandal, scraping down with a strigil after exercise and oiling (*18*). The last subject we shall meet again on an Etruscan scarab (*123*) in a more advanced style with one leg frontal, not both profile as here.

Few Archaic scarabs are inscribed. Artists are usually precise and neat in their signatures. When a name is added boldly in the field, with the letters fitting around the figure as best they may, as on *21*, we may suspect that the Moschos here was the owner who had his name added to the intaglio. There is another scaraboid, *23*, of rock crystal – not a material in which the intaglio is easily viewed without an impression, and certainly not one worth cutting into a meticulous scarab beetle shape rather than a blocked-out scaraboid. The slimmer, more upright figure indicates a date already within the fifth century, but here we may take the second Archaic masterpiece (*22*), the youth stooping to fasten his sandal, leaning on his stick, in a pose whose popularity on gems of around 500 BC has already been explained. The strong legs, the sure detailing of hair, features and body, together with the superb sense of balance and composition of the single figure in the long oval field – not an easy pose in art or life – betray a master's hand. To demonstrate fully the quality of the cutting I show both stone and impression twice, with different lighting. In several Greek gems with studies of youths in this general style the works of at least three masters can be detected, and of these I am inclined to attribute the scarab here to the most famous, who is also the only one to have left us his name – Epimenes. He signs a gem in Boston, with a youth restraining a horse, and certainly his work is a gem in New York with a youth testing an arrow. Both display three-quarter twisting views of their backs, a pose few sculptors of the day would have attempted. A third stone in Boston, with a youth drawing a bow, has the same view of the back, but the rest of the body is less finely marked. Compare the heads and limbs on these stones with our sandal-binder and the identity of hand seems certain. The pose here is less challenging, but the artist has accurately rendered the three-quarter chest and the sinking right shoulder, where his contemporaries, faced with a comparable figure, preferred to pull the chest round frontal. Epimenes' other gems are scaraboids: this is a scarab of a common Greek type with a ridged back, carefully but not elaborately cut. The tiny heads on these Archaic stones may seem to offer slight opportunity for attribution to individual artists, and we have, of course, to rely on other criteria of anatomy, pose, and general style. However, the finest artists betray themselves even in microscopic detail, and on page 80 I have assembled enlarged photographs of heads from impressions of scarabs by the leading recognized Archaic masters. The place of our scarab with the Epimenes gems seems assured, both for the similarity of the youth's head, and its marked difference from the head-type favoured by the hardly less talented contemporary Semon Master, eight of whose heads are also shown together with one or two others to provide further comparative contrasts. It must be recalled that on the original stones the heads shown here are only two to three millimetres high and the enlargements are therefore ten to fifteen times. A is from the signed Epimenes stone. B is from the New York stone attributed to him mainly for the body modelling, but the head is very similar, though more detailed, being larger. C is the third stone associated with Epimenes, mainly for the body posture; it is less detailed work but the physiognomy is basically the same as for A and B. D is from our stone, clearly intermediate between A and C and giving coherence to the group. E is from an incomplete stone in Boston with a youth stooping to pick up a helmet. The style of the head is closely related to D, but not the same, nor is the body. By contrast F (a girl) is from the name-piece of the Semon Master. Notice the higher cheek, flatter skull and the nose turning up rather than with the Epimenean bulbous tip (especially on C and D). G (Eros and a girl), H (youth held by a griffin) and J (youth held by a sphinx) repeat the Semon Master's heads, as do the bearded heads, K (Herakles fights the lion) and L (winged man-bull), especially for the noses and the eyes (compare J and L). M to P are from other late Archaic stones to demonstrate that, despite the overall similarity, these tiny works can still betray the individuality of separate artists.

We return to the new Epimenes gem whose subject is worth a second look. The youth is fastening his sandal – a motif seen on a number of other Archaic stones although rarely in just this pose. Since only one sandal is shown it is tempting to recall mythical occasions on which one sandal was worn, as by Jason on his arrival at Iolkos. Here, however, the advantages of this pose, already remarked, probably suggested the motif, and although a stock theme may become identified with myth (arming men and Achilles, etc.) we should look for some further clue to identity before attaching any significance to the absence of the other sandal (not yet picked up: already removed?), and no such clue is apparent. On two other gems a sandal-adjuster is an athlete, holding an aryballos. On an Etruscan gem the youth is named Theseus, who had recovered his father's sandals, but Etruscan inscribed scarabs are not a reliable guide to Greek iconography, and on this one both sandals are shown.

The remaining Archaic scarabs carry animal subjects. The goat on *24* could easily pass as the work of the Master of the London Satyr, for although the beetle back is poorer the stippled hide, eye and springy legs are closely matched in his works. The lioness with cub on *26* also appears in his work, but here the treatment of the body is more advanced, although the head is awkwardly conceived. The joined lion and boar foreparts (*27*) – a good subject for a gem which can be viewed either way up – and the lion attacking a ram (*28*) are in the Greek Common Style, but the fact that both have a small flower or bud springing from the ground of the scene links them with the Greco-Phoenician scarabs, where just this style is used for the Greek subjects. The ram is a rare quarry for a lion – the fight is not met again on gems. The proud frontal griffin (*25*) is of the new fifth-century variety with a spiky mane.

The Early Classical and Classical periods bring a new range of subjects, generally on large stones of scaraboid shape, but the scarab is not forgotten. Although the frontal eye of the fine woman's head on the tiny stone, *30*, is still Archaic, these single-head studies are more characteristic of the Early Classical. *29* is somewhat less easy to place, though probably Early Classical. It is still in scarab form but most unusual for the extreme depth of the cutting, giving fullest value to the menacing lion head. Coins with this motif take a top view and avoid the problem of the projecting muzzle and gaping jaw. This head recalls the marble heads from the Temple of Zeus at Olympia and the date may be near. The two mice playing below it are unexpected and might be later additions. There were several animal fables about the lion and the mouse, usually to the credit of the latter.

31 is one of the larger blue scaraboids, and here, as on many Classical stones, the hatched border to the intaglio is abandoned. There are not many two-figure groups on Classical stones and this one is novel for gems. The style of the naked body, drapery and frontal face is matched on other Classical gems. The motif of a satyr stealing upon a sleeping nymph was a popular Archaic one on vases, and it survives, notably with the unveiling gesture, for figures of sleeping Ariadne revealed to Dionysos. But this should be a maenad weary from the dance, sleeping on a rock, her thyrsos wand laid aside. On vases of this period the maenad commonly still holds her thyrsos and her dress is not disturbed, but the setting is usually rocky and the position of the arms is easily matched.

The horseman jumping from his horse on *34* appears on another example of the blue chalcedony scaraboids, the commonest Classical material and shape (in the Archaic period cornelian and scarabs were preferred). The motif was a military exercise, and is seen also on sixth-century scarabs. There are several representations of it in Western Greek art, and the closest to this, with the youth's bent leg and spear, appears on contemporary coins of Himera in Sicily (as our *Fig. 2*). Our gem might be Western Greek too: the cutting and proportions are not wholly assured.

Another comparison with Sicilian coins is invited by *36*, which might seem on further investigation to require a Western Greek studio, but there are problems. Aphrodite rides her goose. On late fifth-century coins of Kamarina the local nymph rides a swimming swan (our *Fig. 3*), raising her dress like a sail. Our bird is the thicker necked goose, and the dress less obviously an aid to progress. The bird appears to be flying, but the trailing legs are omitted and it could be that the device is copied from a swimming goose. A fine contemporary bronze mirror from Eretria (our *Fig. 1*) shows Aphrodite on her swan's back, motionless, feeding it from a bowl but holding her dress over her head as here (see also below, on the ring *78*). The head and three-quarter foot are well observed and rendered, but the weak, straight wing-feathers and absent legs, which may be a matter of mis-calculation, might argue an apprentice hand here.

Busts and half figures are generally foreign to Classical art, so the half maenad on *32*, naked, her head thrown back in ecstasy or song, is rather unexpected. With it, somewhere in Turkey, was said to have been found *33*, a barrel-shaped gem with one side shaved flat for the intaglio, in the Greek manner. Agate is the commonest material for this rare class, most of which are of the best Classical period, and there is another, larger example with a lioness, from Tarentum (our *Fig. 7*). With these gems, presumably in a tomb, were alleged to be found various stone beads and five metal fibulae (brooches), their pins and catch-plates missing, decorated with bone figures of birds (*Fig. 5*).

The Athena of *35* must represent a statue, and there are hints of a base. The zigzags on the skirt enhance the archaizing effect. A similar, finer Athena statue is seen on a contemporary cornelian scaraboid in Boston (our *Fig. 9*).

38 is mainly remarkable for the subject, which is commoner on ringstones. *39* is in a finely mottled jasper which had been popular with some of the better Classical artists, including Dexamenos; but this takes us into the fourth century with its huntress Artemis and her torch, the subject of a statue of her made by Praxiteles for Antikyra, and in a pose rather like this if later coins of Antikyra are a good guide, but with her dog beside her. Earlier, Strongylion had made one of her holding two torches. The letters AΔ, set large and crudely in the field, may refer to the owner, although the same two are seen on the finer, somewhat earlier stone in Boston (*Fig. 9*), where they are set discreetly on the base of a statue of Athena, and more probably refer to the artist.

Gems with their backs cut in the form of a reclining lion were the only type of figure seal admitted in the Classical period apart from the scarab beetle. *37* can be added to the dozen or more already known. A lion gem had been familiar in the east long before (as our *211*), and in Archaic Greece, especially in ivory. There is one Late Archaic example in cornelian, forerunner of the main series which belongs to the fourth century. Ours has been damaged by fire.

Classical gems carry some of the finest known animal studies in Greek art. The duck on *41* is an oddity, but the pigeon on *40*, with a small bundle hanging from its beak, is a fine study of a rising bird. There is a poorer replica of the bird in Boston, thought to be carrying a scroll. Carrier pigeons these may be, for they were known in antiquity, but they would not have carried the messages in their beaks like this, and it is an oddly unrealistic way of depicting their functions. A third version, in a private collection in Switzerland (our *Fig. 8*), makes clear that the bird is carrying a ribbon or fillet, which is shown at full length with its fastening cords at either end. The ribbon may symbolize a victory, but the specific reference in these gems eludes us, and rolled ribbons appear on funeral monuments. On our and the Boston gems the ribbon is rolled and fastened.

The goat, *42*, is a superb successor to that on the Archaic scarab (*24*), although the shape of the stone is a puzzle – not a scaraboid, nor the usual shape for a ringstone of the type beginning to become fashionable. The detailing of the anatomy is perhaps too emphatic for the full Classical, where the forms are muted (compare *43*), and this comes close still to the best Late Archaic animal studies. It is a fine blend of Archaic pattern, especially in the pose, and observation of natural forms. The stone was possibly a trial piece, but by a master, and the poor border to the field may have been added later. Other animal studies are later and of more familiar types (*43–48*).

The lion part of the chimaera on *49* matches the best of the late fifth century, but the puny forepart of a goat at its back, gasping fire, looks rather like an afterthought. Notice how the Greek engraver defines the claws where the Greco-Persian studios leave them as knobbly drill-holes (as on *100*). The smaller, rounder heads are characteristic of Classical lions and feeding-time scenes, such as *50*. This is a cornelian scarab, a late use of the shape for Greece, the border of the intaglio reduced to a line where most Classical stones dispense with a border altogether, although there is a lingering use of the hatched border. The blue chalcedony scaraboids are more typical of the period, and the same material is used for the ringstone preserved here with its mount (*51*). For some fourth-century scaraboids the intaglios were cut on the convex backs, not the flat bases, and the curved surface was preferred for Greek ringstones. This is a simple, not the very finest study of a stag, which was a popular subject on the scaraboids, (as *46*). The heavy ring shape is early Hellenistic.

Before we leave the Classical gems we may notice some in poorer material – glass. Most of the fifth and fourth century are like flat scaraboids, of pale green glass with some, generally early, of clear glass. They could be mass produced from moulds, themselves often manufactured from better stones, but sometimes the devices are cut direct in the glass. The simpler head and animal devices are often repeated. I choose from several in this collection one with a commonplace device, a head (*52*), to show how even on a comparatively well preserved specimen

110

39

121

22

56

127

115

B

the smooth surface is damaged by time and burial. This is a rarity, however, since it is in blue glass, more common in Phoenician than Greek studios. And a finer specimen, shown in impression, of which one replica is known, with Diomedes kneeling, sword drawn, clutching the Palladion cult image of Athena he has just stolen from her sanctuary in Troy (*53*).

In Hellenistic Greece the common gem shape is the ringstone, a long oval, with a marked convex face and not pierced. Ringstones were not unfamiliar in Greek lands earlier, and the fourth-century tendency to carve scaraboids on their convex backs instead of the flat base has already been noticed. *55* is a late example of such a scaraboid, with a Nike carrying a trophy in a type which is to have a long life into the early Roman period. *56, 57* are examples of the normal Hellenistic type of ringstone, with the characteristic elongated figures. The ancient clay impression *58* is typical of a class met on various South Italian sites. It is not a sealing but may have been used for casting glass intaglios or simply as a counter, curio or record of the stone from which it was made. The device is interesting – Eros armed with Zeus' thunderbolt. Alcibiades was said to have had such a figure as the device on his shield, but with the bolt poised like a spear. This is a very early representation of the motif.

Cameos are an invention of the Hellenistic period, but I illustrate here none from the collection. They exploit the varicoloured layers of onyx, but beside them are examples of shallow relief gems in stone of uniform colour. One such is *59*, a minute bust portrait of a Hellenistic queen, almost certainly Berenike II of Egypt.

CHAPTER II

Rings

All-metal finger rings – signet rings of the type familiar today – are rare in Greece and Greek lands before the sixth century BC. In the Archaic period they appear in a variety of forms, in gold or silver, but generally of flimsy construction and probably never used for sealing but worn as jewellery. This remains true through the Classical period, especially for rings of precious metal, although to judge from surviving sealings or objects impressed by rings, bronze rings were more commonly employed as signets, and by the end of the Classical period stones were more often set immobile in finger rings, instead of being set as pendants, and they are used for sealing.

The majority of the rings in this collection are certainly of Western Greek origin: the Archaic ones mainly from Sicily (Selinus), the Classical from Sicily and South Italy, especially Tarentum. Although the Western Greek contribution to stone gem engraving seems to have been slight it does seem likely that the colonies had studios making metal rings, generally of silver, before the full Classical period, and this collection makes it possible to define more closely what shapes and subjects they favoured. The silver rings, *60–69*, are probably all Late Archaic, of the second half of the sixth century BC. Closer dating is not possible.

We start with the least common – the two hoop rings, *60* and *61*, with which can be taken a comparable silver ring of unknown provenience in London (our *Fig. 11*). These introduce the range of animal types preferred on the western rings – the common Archaic lions, birds and horse, but a special interest too in odder figures – beetle, fly, frog and tortoise – such as are also chosen at other times and places for the devices of gems and rings. An odd choice we might think, but Pheidias himself was celebrated for his gems showing a cicada, a fly and a bee (and compare our *77*). A gorgoneion as on *62* is uncommon as a ring device although often chosen to fill a circular field elsewhere in Greek art. The snake heads holding the bezel are found on other rings (as our *63* and compare *76*) and are especially appropriate for a Gorgon ring.

The rings with long diamond bezels, curving with the hoop which is made of a bar bent and brazed together and not cast whole, are the commonest and already quite well represented in the west. These (*64–67*) add more odd motifs – a lobster and a spider. The style is exactly that of the hoop rings and all could easily come from a single studio.

The broader and flatter bezel of *68* (as that of *69*) presents the stirrup shape which survives into the fifth century. It could, however, easily be the earliest ring here, since the drooping wing for Pegasus is an old orientalising motif and unexpected on what must still be a sixth-century ring. The gold stud on the bezel appears on several Archaic and Classical silver rings and is thought to have had some magical significance. *69* is another comparatively primitive bezel, with another orientalising subject, and this time with two gold studs inset.

With the fifth century the leaf shaped bezel became established as the normal type for metal finger rings, broadening gradually to a full oval, and in the fourth century to a circle. A new range of figure types is found, fewer animals, more devoted to studies of deities and especially to studies of Aphrodite with Eros. We may assume that the rings in precious metal were more favoured now as jewellery by women. It is still possible to detect Western Greek studios, some of them represented here. The Victory (Nike) on *70* is commonplace but rather heavier rings have finer subjects. *71* is still Archaic in style. Herakles loses his beard more often in Late Archaic Greek art and is more often shown at ease. Here he has laid aside his club and reclines, with a cup. Compare the vigorous anatomy of our stone intaglio, *1*, but the cutting in the gold is coarser, more direct.

73, 74 and *75* are fine Classical rings. *73*, from Tarentum, is exceptionally fine in detail and unusual in subject – a woman, part naked, seated, holding a floral spray. Her seat appears to be the upper part of an Ionic column with its capital, rather than an altar. A similar support for figures, usually divinities, can be found on gems and rings of this period, but it is a surprising one since this is not the period for ruins to serve as picturesque furniture. With *74* we are certainly facing Western Greek work – there is a replica, omitting the Eros, from Tarentum (our *Fig. 10*). And *75* is from the same studio as rings from Tarentum which show a similar winged woman, similarly coiffed. She is not Nike but perhaps a local nymph like the one figured on contemporary coins of Terina (in South Italy; as our *Fig. 4*). On the other rings she carries a caduceus, binds a sandal, and seems naked, kneeling on a column. The Eros with her here suggests that she may have been assimilated to Aphrodite.

The lighter ring, *76*, is mainly remarkable for showing Herakles as an athlete, an oil bottle in his hand by his club, and for the ring's open hoop with snake head ends.

With the fourth century the large, flat, oval or round bezels become the rule. Quality varies enormously. The only interest in *79* lies in its subject, Aphrodite weighing two erotes in a balance, and the fact that she is seated, not standing, as we would expect for this subject. *82* presents the Classical Hellenistic Medusa head, all human now (contrast our *3*, *8* and *62*) but for the wings and snakes in her hair.

78 is probably full Hellenistic, a fine large bezel showing a goddess feeding a swan. The scheme is as that for Ganymede, seated on rocks, feeding Zeus' eagle. I have argued elsewhere that this episode, commonly shown in early Roman art, may as well refer to the lad's seduction by the Zeus eagle as to his serving it in Olympus, and compared how Leda was tricked into helping the apparently frightened Zeus swan. The two stories were associated in Roman art and in Greek epigram (*Anth. Pal. v, 65*), and we find the Ganymede feeding the eagle beside the seduction of Leda on single monuments. It is tempting, therefore, to identify the figure on the ring as Leda and to deduce that both theme and iconography are related to the Ganymede episodes. We cannot be sure of this, however, without other representations where a Leda is more certainly identified. Other ladies have dealings with swans. It was Aphrodite's bird. She is shown riding it from the early fifth century on in Greek art, and on the fine bronze mirror of the late fifth century (our *Fig. 1*) which we have already noticed, she contrives to feed it from a bowl while on its back. The feeding motif is established, then, for Aphrodite, and in early Roman art Venus is seen with an eagle, once feeding it, but the poses are again different. Another related motif is of Hygieia feeding her snake from a cup or horn, as it appears on two remarkable intaglios from Pompeii, but here the goddess is standing. The case for Leda must then rest on the clear relationship to the Ganymede and eagle scenes. It is not known whether the ring was found in Sicily but there was another patroness of swans there, the nymph Kamarina, whose possible relationship to another gem in this collection has already been discussed.

Of the fourth – or third-century bronze rings which seem to have been commonly used for sealing, I show only one with Eros, possibly playing with a love charm

Fig. 1

Fig. 2

Fig. 3

Fig. 4

Fig. 6

Fig. 5

Fig. 7

Fig. 8

Fig. 9

Fig. 10

Fig. 11

Fig. 12

Fig. 14

Fig. 13

Fig. 15

Fig. 16

Fig. 17

Fig. 18

Fig. 19

Fig. 20

(*80*). *81* is probably of the same date despite its oval bezel. It is remarkable both for its subject – birds on a laver – and the use of the tremolo technique for the patterns on the bowl, base and border. This zigzag of arcs was produced by rocking a chisel-like tool to and fro along the surface. The technique had been used extensively on Geometric Greek bronzes and some ivories, but survives in Greek lands only for details on gold jewellery, as here.

CHAPTER III

Greeks, Persians and Phoenicians

The role of the east in the history of Greek gem engraving was an important one with the Greeks as pupils, learning new techniques, new forms, new motifs. With the advent of Persians in Aegean affairs the relationship changes, and the gems which illustrate this chapter show the effect of Greek styles within the Persian Empire and in areas where they had themselves learnt the new scarab forms and the techniques of cutting hard stones and which now supplied Phoenician markets in the east and in the western Mediterranean.

In the middle of the sixth century the Persian king Cyrus crushed Lydia, seized Croesus in his court at Sardis, and brought Persian arms to the shores of the Aegean. For the following two centuries, until Alexander, the Greek cities and islands of the coastline lived through periods of independence or of changing, even mixed allegiances to the empires of Athens or of Persia. The Lydia of Croesus had been permeated by Greek manners and art. Coinage had been invented there a half century before, perhaps by Greeks, and its use spread quickly through the Greek (not the eastern) world and was learned by the Persians. Sardis became the capital of a new Persian province, with a Persian govenor's court. Seal use was important to the easterners. At Sardis they used the eastern cylinder (as *85*) and particularly the pyramidal, eight-sided stamp seal – an older Assyrian and Babylonian shape (as *83*, *84*, *86*). They are often supplied with gold or silver hoop mounts, with duck-head terminals, and for these the stones are not pierced right through. The intaglios carry formal Persian motifs, of king-heroes or monsters, but some are in a style closer to the Archaic Greek and even borrow Greek themes. Those shown here are in the Achaemenid Persian Court style but include subjects of unusual interest. The lion fighting a bull (*83*) is a common enough subject in the east and on these gems, but it is rendered here with the bull in a realistic pose, its hind leg trailing, more familiar in Greek art. The body markings are purely Persian, but contrast the stiff formality of the relief group at Persepolis. Mixed monsters, like that on *84*, are another speciality of this class (compare our *Fig. 12*). The boar's forepart may derive from more explicit views of a monster holding a boar as prey beneath its forepaws (our *Fig. 13*). The basic monster – a goat-horned, human headed lion (a goat-sphinx) is familiar enough, but look closely at its wing. It takes the form of a rampant lion, its body marked to suggest feathering. This is unique, but explicable in terms of other eastern representations, where we may see a wing terminating in an animal head (the probable origin of the goat element in the Greek chimaera), and especially on a series of mixed animal and human head motifs which are current in Phoenician art of this period and which appear on some Achaemenid finger rings. In these one or more human heads are combined with animal heads, often including a boar's forepart, but the ear, beard and neckline of the main bearded head is replaced by the whole body of a water bird (as our *Fig. 16*). The principle is exactly that of the lion here masquerading as a wing. On Greco-Phoenician scarabs there are other varieties of this treatment, with a dolphin serving as the head of a water bird analogous to the Scythian translation of parts of animals into other animal forms and all these phenomena may own the same origin in eastern art. The Greeks would not usually go beyond using an animal head as a terminal to a device, but not normally on any animal figure.

The seals of Persian Lydia are a special phenomenon in the Persian Empire, not matched even elsewhere in their western satrapies. Most of the seals seem to belong to the later sixth and early fifth centuries, contemporary with later Archaic Greek gems. The main Greco-Persian series of gems, however, corresponds with the Greek Classical, and so far as we can judge they were being produced mainly in the later fifth and early fourth century in the southern satrapies of Asia Minor and perhaps in Syria, not in Lydia.

The world portrayed on the Greco-Persian gems is a court life of Persian nobles seen through Greek eyes in the conventions of theme and composition which are natural to Greek, not eastern art. Technically they are Greek in the preference shown for large scaraboids and for flat surfaces, which is probably why tabloids (like *89*) were favoured rather than cylinders or the eastern stamp seals with convex faces. Compositions are Greek in their preference for single or simple figure groups. In detail of execution their origin outside the Greek world is betrayed

by markings on animals which may come close to the stylisations of the Achaemenid Court Style, and a willingness to let simple drilling and cuts speak for
themselves, notably on animal bodies, limbs and feet, where the Greek artist at
home took pains to disguise all clues to technique and achieved a style exactly
comparable with that of larger subjects in other materials. Many Greco-
Persian gems are frankly summary and lack the discipline and skill of the Greek
studios, but still achieve a lively and decorative effect.

Court life in the east is expressed in art through elaborate scenes of ritual,
parade and tribute bearing, but on the Greco-Persian gems we are, characteris-
tically for Greeks, allowed to view the off-duty behaviour of these princes. The
atmosphere is, of course, different from that of contemporary Athenian art, with
its emphasis on the boudoir, the palaistra or the battlefield. It is a more virile,
open air, country gentleman style, such as Xenophon approved both on his
Peloponnesian estates and for Persian princes. We see Persians with their women,
who bring them flowers or oil. The women may be on their own, with their
children or dogs – domestic scenes unknown in eastern art, especially with the
greater intimacies which are also sometimes admitted on the gems. The men are
dressed for hunting in their trousered, sleeved costume and over-tunic, muffled
in the soft Persian cap. The women are buxom, pig-tailed, in loose flowing gowns
like the Greek chiton. The active life is that of the hunt, on horseback or on foot,
often with dogs, after all manner of wild beasts – lions, antelopes, wild goats and
bulls, bears, even foxes. The lions recall the more formal scenes of king-hero
grappling a lion (as on *85*), but these lion hunts are as real as Alexander's. And
many other gems show the quarry alone at full flying gallop, or brought down and
torn by dogs or birds. These are the hunting prints of antiquity. When our
Persian has to fight it is usually against Greeks, and there are the occasional single
studies of a Greek warrior. Of monsters, only the griffin, a favourite east and west,
appears regularly in single studies.

Xenophon we have mentioned already: an Athenian, who campaigned long for
Greeks and for the Persian Cyrus in Asia Minor, for and through those provinces
in which the Greco-Persian gems were apparently being made and worn. Exiled
from Athens he was given an estate near Olympia, but returned home to die in
about 354 B.C., over seventy years old. His career and literary interests provide a
background to the world of the gems. He wrote a treatise on hunting; another on
the ideal education of a Persian prince, humanely authoritarian with an emphasis
on the character-building qualities of physical fitness and the hunting field; and
studies in history, politics, economics, and horsemanship.

We learn something from him of Greek hunting habits and can the better then
understand how different are those of the gems. Greece is not a place for hunting

215

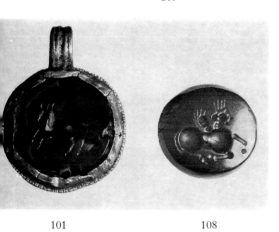

101   108

101   4

209   87

on horseback, and the treatises on hunting, including Xenophon's, are devoted mainly to care of the hounds and the tactics of hunting on foot, with dogs, snares and nets. The plains of North Greece and of Anatolia gave better opportunities. From the mid sixth century on, mounted hunters pursuing stags appear on some Greek vases but they are mainly East Greek and when they are seen on Athenian vases the motif is merely borrowed, and not the local hunting practice. The East Greeks would have known about mounted hunts in the plains and valleys of Western Anatolia. Farther east we learn from documents and reliefs of the parks for wild animals managed for the Assyrian kings. Here the hunting was on horseback or from chariots, and the parks – the Greeks called them paradises (*paradeisoi*) – are found in Anatolia in the Persian period. Xenophon knew these parks both in his service with the Persians and during his epic march with the Ten Thousand which took him through some of the provinces where the Greco-Persian gems were made. He has little to tell us about Persian hunting habits, however, beyond mention of the parks, and the description of an episode when Cyrus, stag hunting, met a boar (*Cyropaedia* i, 4.4). One of the commonest hunts which we learn about from the gems may seem familiar enough – fox-hunting on horseback; not, however, with hounds but with a trident-tipped lance. Plutarch tells us that Alexander himself went fox-hunting during his travels through Asia, no doubt in this manner. The Persian horses wear saddle cloths, as we can see from *89*, and so did the East Greek hunters shown on black figure vases. With no fixed saddle and no stirrups eastern hunting called for the finest horsemanship.

The Greco-Persian gems of this collection illustrate many of the themes which have been mentioned. We may single out the typical family group, *87*, and the unique dancer on *88*, celebrating, it may be, a good day's hunting. The Greeks knew this eastern dance, with hands clasped over the head and body swaying from side to side, and they often show it performed by men or women in eastern dress in Classical art, for instance on the red figure vase, our *Fig. 20*. But popular dances are not fit subjects for eastern art and this gem is the closest we get to an eastern representation of it. It is tempting to identify this dance as the *Persikon* mentioned by Aristophanes (*Thesm. 1175*), which his scholiast explains as the *oklasma*, a dance in which squatting is apparently involved. In some of the Greek representations of the eastern dances with arms raised the figures are crouching. Xenophon (*Anab. vi, 1.10*) describes a similar dance, performed by a Mysian. In this two shields are held, there is spinning and squatting, and the finale is the *Persikon*. Much later Heliodoros (*Aethiop. iv, 17*) describes an Assyrian mode with jumping, squatting, and spinning round. We are clearly dealing with a common form of eastern dance where the dancers spin round with hands over their head or holding shields, dropping to their haunches from time to time, much like the latter-day

C

whirling Dervishes. It is the spinning posture which is shown most commonly on Greek vases, where the dress may be seen to be flying out, and on our gem.

The tabloid *89* can be added to the ten others known of this distinctive shape and decorated in this manner. The main scene is a lion hunt; on the shoulders are coursing animals – fox, bear, antelope and bull; on the back, the pet dog. The group on the large flat scaraboid *90* is not merely a scene of the hunting field, to be taken with others showing a dead animal being torn (as *Fig. 14*), but harks back to a far older oriental theme of one or two birds at the body of an animal, which was current also on the pyramidal stamp seals of Sardis, where the repertory was formal Achaemenid and not genre. This is a clear indication that the Greco-Persian gems cannot simply be explained as the work of Greeks for new masters, since this shows a fuller understanding of older eastern iconography.

Many Greco-Persian scaraboids are devoted simply to the animals of the chase, shown running or quiet (*94–96*), with a few of the traditional groups of lions or griffins fighting other beasts (*97*) which had symbolic significance for easterners. The griffins are hellenised by now, crested, and unusually *100* has still the Archaic forehead knob, but we have two, deviant, wingless griffins too (*98, 99*). There is some variety of animals shown in this collection, including a unique representation of a striped hyena (*92*), a beast often shown on its own on these gems, once wounded, but never actually being hunted, and a nicely observed, though summarily cut, horse nibbling its fetlock, *93*.

Greek influence on gem engraving in the Persian Empire was confined to the west, and especially Asia Minor, through its main period, but towards its end, when Greek arms led by Alexander the Great penetrated the Empire to its heart, we find successors to the Greco-Persian stones in the Persian homeland itself. A group of scaraboids which I have called the Bern Group, presents many of the Greco-Persian motifs in a looser style, with some Greek features about the protagonists – the dressing of the horses' tails (or lack of it), the men's costumes and caps – which suggests that these are Alexander's Macedonians living as Persian nobles, in Persia and in the eastern provinces. The style is looser, and lapses into a treatment of undisguised drill work (a globolo – *107–109*: compare the Etruscan of a later chapter). These, at least, seem current also in the western empire, but here purely Greek Hellenistic styles of gem engraving, on ringstones, were to persist. In the east, to the borders of India, the last of the old Greco-Persian style was to linger and to influence far later gems in this distant area.

Many of the Bern Group scaraboids are smaller, rounder, sometimes not pierced or with a very thin perforation for fastening to a rigid mount rather than a swivel. *101* is a precious example of how they might be set as pendants, and not stringed on a necklet or hoop. The palmette pattern on the gold back is Greek, early Hellenistic. Other stones give poor versions of the older hunts and animal studies (*102, 103, 105, 106*). Reclining animals are often preferred now, and the flying gallop is not forgotten. The sphinxes are Greek, female with smooth round faces (*108, 109*), but they wear what seems to be a version of the old Achaemenid crown which had been worn also by the Persian, bearded, male sphinxes and is also worn by women on gems of this class. *104* is the only example of this series known to me which shows elephants, beasts which Alexander's Greeks first met in battle on the Hydaspes, and which became more familiar in Hellenistic Greece and its armies.

The other series of gems of the Persian period on which Greek and eastern motifs and styles are mixed is very different in appearance and distribution. Before the mid-sixth century Greek studios, perhaps in Cyprus, learned from Phoenicians to work hard stone and cut scarab seals, as we have already seen. Down to this date Phoenician scarabs had been of various materials and the commonest carried strongly Egyptianising motifs of deities and monsters or inscriptions. After this date, and through most of the period of Persian domination, the favourite material becomes green jasper, and to the Egyptianising subjects are added others with local subjects (a Baal or Melkart) or with purely Greek subjects, usually of Late Archaic type. Where other materials are used, the types tend to remain traditional, Egyptianising. These scarabs are found in Syria, Phoenicia and Cyprus, but are far more common in the western Mediterranean, on Phoenician and Punic sites, in Spain, on Ibiza and Sardinia, and in Carthage itself. It is not yet clear whether any, or if so which, were made in the west. There is full agreement in shapes and motifs at either end of the inland sea.

There is good reason to believe that the green jasper scarabs in this collection may be from sites in western Sicily, such as Motya, and so attest the currency of the type in a Punic area which has so far yielded a very few from excavation, as well as clay sealings from similar scarabs found in the Greek colony at Selinus. The fact that several of these scarabs are unusually small and in a distinctive dark stone also suggests some coherence in the group.

We have already seen one version of the god Bes fighting a lion on *7*, and in a fine gold setting which is matched also on Punic sites. It is a more authentic Bes who appears on the green jasper *110*, more finely detailed and with a knobbly anatomy which recalls Archaic Greek intaglios rather than anything eastern. His adversary is a griffin of eastern type, with crest and no mane, and in the field we see the eastern crescent and disc symbol and the Egyptian coiled cobra (*uraeus*). This is the best Late Archaic style of the jasper scarabs. The Bes with a lion on *111* is, however, in the commoner style for this class, and others, with Egyptian

35

(*113*, Horus enthroned) or eastern (*112*, Baal on a sphinx-throne) subjects are even more summary.

Others owe more to Greek inspiration. Herakles with the lion was a popular motif in this class, since the Greek hero was readily assimilated to the eastern Melkart, but the preferred pose for the fight is the eastern, standing one. On *115* he kneels to wrestle with the lion in a pose invented for the combat by Greek artists in the second half of the sixth century and shown often on Athenian vases. All that is changed, or that is perhaps misunderstood here, is that Herakles is kneeling, with knees together, and without one leg carried forward. The group is easier to understand like this, at this small scale. This is the only example of this scheme for the fight in this series. The satyr on *114* is purely Greek, East Greek by breed to judge by his horse's feet. The pose is close to that on several Archaic Greek scarabs (and compare the Etruscan *122*) but the detail rougher.

The fight on *116* is an Egyptian and eastern scheme with the victim reduced in size and seized by his hair, but here the victor is not an eastern king or hunter, but a Greek warrior and his victim an old man. It is not clear whether a particular story was in mind or the motif has simply been hellenised. On *117*, far poorer work, the fisherman with trident and fish is probably to be identified as an easterner, although his pose is that of a youthful Greek Poseidon. The head on *118* is not remarkable but the back view of a horse on *119* is. This unusual viewpoint was one favoured in later Archaic Greek art and occurs sometimes on the Greco-Punic scarabs and rings. Finally, the scarab with a chimaera on *120* is not in green jasper but a mottled serpentine. The style and material is represented in Tharros on Sardinia, and likely to have been made there. The way the goat's head appears to grow from a wing on the lion's body recalls the probable origin for this feature in the Greek chimaera (see also above, on *84*) and is represented in this explicit way often in Etruscan art.

It is not certain whether the green jasper scarabs were still being made in the fourth century BC, but this is the last important series of engraved scarabs in antiquity with the Egyptian and eastern intaglios which are natural to the form. This is not, however, the end of the history of the scarab, for in the hands of another western Mediterranean people, the Etruscans, it was to survive until new Greek styles in Italy, serving Rome's new role as the centre of empire, dismissed them as a working seal form. To the Etruscan scarabs we turn now.

CHAPTER IV

Etruscan Scarabs

The fascination of Etruscan art lies in the way it combines a Greek idiom with a robustly and strictly un-Classical view of life, myth and religion. Etruscan scarabs have played an important part in the study of Etruscan art largely because so many have survived – perhaps three thousand – and have therefore long been accessible to connoisseurs and collectors in Italy, and this is probably the result of their popularity in antiquity, as jewellery rather than for sealing purposes. The Etruscans became familiar with scarabs in the second half of the sixth century through the import of Greek stones and then by the establishment in Etruria of immigrant Greek studios. At this time the important studios for scarabs in the Greek world were all located on the east of the Aegean, from Ionia to Cyprus. Persia was threatening in these years, and many Greek towns owed allegiance to the Great King. Many East Greeks sought new homes and their emigrant artists played an important, in fact a decisive role in the development of what we recognize as Archaic Etruscan art. This is as true of gem engraving as it is of vase painting or sculpture. The styles and subject repertory of the first new studios were to play an influential part in the later history of Etruscan scarab engraving, a symptom of the common conservative tendencies in other Etruscan crafts. The works of these new studios are easily identified from about 500 BC on, but in the earlier years the problems of distinguishing Greek imported from Greek 'made in Etruria' are not light. One gem in this collection is an important addition to the known work of an artist who, although perhaps Greek by training (in Greece or

Etruria), represents for us the first 'Etruscan' scarab artist. Closer consideration of this can precede more general remarks about the nature and history of Etruscan scarabs and of other examples in a collection which, being mainly formed in Italy, is naturally rich in this class.

The scarab (*121*) is a very small one, barely seven millimetres long, of cornelian. The beetle back is finely detailed with bulbous head, carefully feathered wings incised on the wing cases (*elytra*) and equally carefully modelled legs. The sides of the plinth or base on which the beetle stands and beneath which the intaglio is cut, are plain. These are all features to be remarked on further below. It is enough here to notice that most Greek scarab beetles are more poorly fashioned, and that the jewellery aspect of the stone may already be apparent.

The device has a dot border, another speciality for Etruria, and the cross hatching below the ground line which goes back to the Phoenician pattern for scarabs as learnt by Greeks. A warrior is arming, clipping a greave to his leg. Before him two spears stand upright, and a man holds a shield for him, when he is ready. Behind him a woman raises her hand in a gesture of welcome or farewell. The central figure is the key one. Look at his feet. From the modelling of the legs it is clear that they 'face' the same way as the man's head, but the feet are cruelly deformed and are twisted back and upwards to small knobbly toes. This must be Hephaistos, the smith god who was lame – a common disability of smiths in mythology – and was explained either as a deformity from which he suffered from birth, or as a result of being thrown down to earth from Olympus by the goddess Hera. As an armourer his most famous commission was to fashion new armour for Thetis to take to her son Achilles at Troy, a replacement for that lost with Patroklos. The woman on our scarab must be Thetis, the warrior Achilles. But the representations of the story in Greek art show Thetis with Hephaistos, Thetis carrying the armour, Thetis giving it to Achilles, and not all three together. Our artist has taken a novel view of the story and we should not be too hasty and say that he has misunderstood it. His other works may help us.

The personality of this artist, whom we call the Master of the Boston Dionysos, was studied in detail first by Professor Zazoff in 1966. This is the seventh stone which can be attributed to his hand. Of the other subjects the important one for us is on a scarab in the Vatican, showing a woman handing armour to a warrior, whom we would naturally take to be Thetis and Achilles. In Florence there is a study of a warrior on his own displaying his armour, no doubt Achilles, but now wearing a 'modern' linen corselet, not the bronze bell corselet. There are also tiny stones in Oxford, Paris and Rome showing youths and a woman. His name piece in Boston replaces the beetle back with a fine relief study of Dionysos, running with his vine. The intaglio (*Fig. 15*) shows Herakles confronting and apparently fighting an old man, watched by Athena and a woman. The action is not clear, the old man's hand is raised in greeting, not supplication, and the gesture of the woman behind him, holding a flower, seems unruffled. But this could be the fight with Nereus, the Old Man of the Sea, lacking attributes but with his wife Doris or patron Hera; or with Geras, Old Age: at all events, another novel treatment of a story.

The master's style is unmistakeable. He loves the fine pointed drill – for toes and details of dress, but he is fairly restrained in his use of it on our scarab. The thickset figures have sinuous outlines, fat thighs and calves, lumpy heels, big heads with strong chins. The physique is matched on other Etruscan works and Zazoff has singled out the Volterra relief stelai. The general style is apparent elsewhere, as at Chiusi or the paintings from Cerveteri or on metalwork. It is the Ionicising style of Etruria in the third quarter of the sixth century. The scarabs cannot be very early to judge from the drapery and details of dress and armour, not necessarily before the 520's BC. We cannot place the studio exactly, nor can we as yet trace clearly the homeland of the style in the east, but we can end this account of the scarab with an observation which relates it to other work in Etruria by an immigrant East Greek artist. It concerns Hephaistos' feet. In Classical Greek art the lameness is generally ignored, but the Archaic artist was not squeamish and enjoyed such details. One way to indicate it, as on the Francois Vase, was to turn one foot back, but there are rare examples too of twisting both feet back and up. One is on a Corinthian vase of the second quarter of the sixth century, and another, which brings the closest parallel to the treatment on our scarab and is contemporary, is on a vase by the Master of the Caeretan Hydriae, a Greek painter whose work is known only on vases painted in and for the Etruscan city of Cerveteri (Caere). Yet a third appears on a dinos of the Northampton/Campana Group, recently acquired by Wurzburg, and apparently with a similar Etruscan – East Greek background. On two of the vases he is beardless, inebriated, riding back to Olympus, not the sober smith of the scarab. The lameness shown in this manner is clearly club foot (*talipes equino-varus*) which must have been observed by Greek artists and, as a congenital deformity, found appropriate for Hephaistos. It is an interesting example of an observation in nature turned to iconographic advantage.

Etruscan scarabs are nearly all made of cornelian. Greek cornelian gems show a variety of colours from dark red to orange, streaky or blotchy. Nearly all the Etruscan are a uniform deep red which might lead one to suspect a single source, used over more than three centuries. It was not, however, a local source and the material probably came in raw lumps from the east or Egypt. Why, then, the difference in colour and its remarkable consistency? It is possible at least that the Etruscans or their suppliers had learnt how to enrich the colour of the stone by heat and other treatment, well enough known to latter-day Indian suppliers but not, it seems, to Pliny, whose book on stones has no word of it.

The value of Etruscan scarabs as jewellery has been remarked. This also explains the rich gold settings and swivels made for the scarabs; and it explains why the artist spent so much time on the beetle back. As much can be learnt of date and development in the scarab series from their backs as from their intaglios. The early scarabs, on into the fourth century, normally have a decorated edge to the plinth (*121* is an early exception, and all the Greek scarabs ignore this element). The little winglets incised on the backs are another early feature, sometimes enhanced by a scroll or palmette, but not outliving the fifth century, it seems. Commoner is a simply cut v at the wing-case corners, a variant on the eastern v markings which appear on the Greek scarab, *1*. This persists into the fourth century. The latest of the Etruscan scarab series, of the fourth and third centuries, simplify further. The backs lose all subtlety of modelling, plinths are plain, legs lightly modelled, or simply incised, and the winglets replaced by one to four oblique cuts. Now too the hatched border to the intaglio is replaced by a single line, or no border at all, and a new style, the a globolo, accounts for the majority, though not from metropolitan Etruria, while finer intaglios nearer the new Greek Hellenistic earn better beetles.

The homes of these studios are not always clearly determined. Most of the main Etruscan series must be from the major cities of Etruria, or some of them, and some of the scarabs are inscribed in Etruscan. The later a globolo are probably from outside Etruria, in Central Italy. The difficulty of isolating Greek work for the early period has been noted, and the quality of some fifth-century work seems to indicate Greek hands, if not outside Etruria. But what of the western Greek colonies? Had they no scarabs? When we find a scarab with Etruscan back inscribed in Greek (in London, Walters, no. 513) we seem to have the answer, but the studios have yet to be found and their works defined. In the later period too the role of Rome and other Italian states cannot be ignored. They seem to have preferred the new, flat ringstones, but so did Etruria from the fourth century on, and only the a globolo gems represent any major continuing scarab production in central Italy.

None of the ringstones of this collection have been selected for illustration here, but a full range of scarabs which demonstrates the variety of styles and subjects, and the rest of this chapter is devoted mainly to the subjects. Many depend still on Archaic themes or poses. Others copy the contemporary Greek, with hesitation. It is their originality which we must seek, since even the most summarily cut may offer a new view of an old story, or a totally new theme whose significance can still challenge us. Behind it all is the lingering knowledge, both that Etruscan artists did not always understand what they borrowed and copied, and that the unfamiliar need not be a matter of misunderstanding since so much of Etruscan art derives from an area of the Greek world whose own iconographic traditions are still little known.

We start with some thoroughly Greek devices. The dancing satyr on *122* has the equine feet common on many East Greek works, including scarabs – an indication of the source of influence for the Etruscan series. The dot border is more favoured in Etruria, but the spirit of this is very close to Greek work (like *1*) and it is easy to imagine that a Greek hand cut this. The athlete scraping his leg with a strigil on *123* is in the stooping posture favoured by the Late Archaic artists in Greece. *18* shows an earlier, Greek version of the motif, with both legs in profile view. While the physique of the warrior on *124* also recalls the Late Archaic of Greece the pose does not. There are many of these collapsing figures on Etruscan scarabs, some of them dropping their sword or helmet, as here. One like ours is labelled Tydeus, one of the heroes who attacked Thebes. Others are called Kapaneus, one of his companions, who was struck by Zeus' thunderbolt. Without inscription or bolt we cannot be sure which, if any, hero was intended here. *127* is an unusually fine stone of the full Classical style. In similar two-figure groups the warrior is more obviously departing, and the pair are twice labelled, Achilles and Odysseus. Here we might rather think of the pensive Achilles with Patroklos armed to go out and fight for the last time. The seated boy's pose, hands clasped around his knee, is an Early Classical one, and it is perhaps surprising to find such a competent rendering of it so soon in Etruscan art. Pausanias (x,31.1) remarks it was used by Polygnotos in his painting in the Cnidian Lesche at Delphi, for Hector in the Underworld, in an attitude of sorrow.

There are a number of winged demons in Etruscan art not all of them identifiable by name or function. On our scarabs we have two women (*125, 126*) and one young male, with cloak, spear and shield (*128*). On these stones we see for the first time that tendency to express figures in terms of the simplest forms offered by the cutting techniques, in grooves and blobs, which becomes dominant in the a globolo style. It was a trait foreign to homeland Greek gem engraving, although not unfamiliar on the hellenising stones of the east. In Italy it appears already in the fifth century, to be most fully developed in the fourth and third. On the earlier stones it accompanies a tendency to blur outlines and the detail which is the hallmark of the best Archaic, but it can also contribute to some striking sculptural effects.

The stooping pose again, on *129*, serves a figure bending towards waves. Similar subjects on scarabs have been variously explained. Tantalos, stretching out for the water he will never reach, is a promising explanation, partly because

41

the water is sometimes shown (as on our *Fig. 18*) as rising in a mass towards him instead of forming the conventional line of waves clinging to the border, partly because other Underworld figures are shown on Etruscan scarabs – Ixion, Sisyphos. On this stone, too, the pebbles shown over the waves make the point that he will never reach the water.

130 presents another problem figure, explained by others as Pelops who won his chariot race with King Oinomaos by contriving to have the king's chariot wheel loosened. Much later Etruscan burial urns with reliefs (second-century BC) show him striking the king with the wheel. Our figure does not seem threatening, and neither his himation cloak nor his shield seem appropriate to the occasion, but I can suggest no other explanation.

132 has another characteristic figure in stooping pose, here, as the Tantalos, with a chlamys cloak at his back. He appears to be placing objects on an altar, but the action and subject are not wholly clear and could be voting with pebbles or even gaming, which would be explicable in terms of Greek myth. *131* is another enigma. The man appears to be removing objects from a pot, or possibly just handling the cords, with which it is to be fastened or sealed. Notice here how the direct, lumpy cutting gives an effective impression of muscled power. The archer, warrior and boot-binder, *133–135*, are nameless. So too the heavy-bodied smith (*137*) unless this is an Hephaistos.

With *138–140* we are on surer ground since the lionskin and clubs should identify Herakles. He is beardless on the first two – as often in the Classical period in both Greek and Etruscan art. On *138* he lifts a massive stone. On another Etruscan scarab he is throwing a boulder into water, perhaps the river Strymon, which he blocked because it impeded his journey. Without the water, we cannot be sure here, and in Etruria Herakles often behaves in a manner not readily matched in Greek art. His association with fountains, for example, as on *139*, is very much an Italian or Western Greek phenomenon. On *140* he is bearded and the style is different, closer to that of fourth-century or later Etruscan ring-stones. The myth at least is clear – his capture of the Stymphalian birds, here rendered in an unusually direct manner rather than in the usual way with him shooting at them. Kapaneus has been mentioned already. On *141* the bolt of Zeus with which he has been struck falls between his legs. The succession of blobs before him, by the edge of the field, is a convention for rocks on other scarabs, but he is shown (on later ringstones, not scarabs) before or on the ladder with which he sought to scale the wall of Thebes, and this may be intended here.

The helmeted head on *142* is again in the style best represented by the later fourth- and third-century ringstones. *143* provides an interesting contrast, with a more purely Greek, Hellenistic treatment of features, possibly to be counted as one of the rare examples of Roman Republican scarabs. A similar solution might be sought for *144*, where the dress and pose of Athena have a Greek freedom and assurance beyond the usual Etruscan or even Italic range for this period. The subject is not the least puzzling feature of this stone – Athena, or at least an armed woman, crowned by Eros with a pose and gesture more familiar from Western Greek representations of him with his mother Aphrodite. Athena's brief amorous encounter with Hephaistos would not have been celebrated thus, but perhaps we should identify her as some other armed goddess – even Aphrodite-Turan. This stone can hardly be later than the third century BC to judge from Eros' apparent age (later he is a baby) and the elaboration of the scarab beetle.

The remaining scarabs are of the a globolo style. They are arranged for illustration and catalogue with, first, those with elaborated beetles (v winglets or real winglets and decorated plinths, *145–169*); then those with simple beetles (oblique winglets and plain legs and plinths, *170–204*). The first can be seen to admit far more linear detail in accessories although the forms of the bodies declare the dominance of technique over style. The second have simpler subjects, often featureless, but still capable of presenting some iconographical problems and surprises. Despite the hundreds of a globolo scarabs known it is still possible to find new subjects upon them, and there are many in the group presented here.

146 shows Daidalos as a winged craftsman plying his adze on a piece of wood. A companion piece in London has him flying holding his adze and a saw (our *Fig. 19*). There had been some doubt about the identification, and the adze had been taken for a throwing stick (*pedum*), the saw for a trap. Our scarab shows the adze in use, however, while on a gold bulla in Baltimore the winged figures on either side, one holding adze and saw, the other a set square and wood axe, are named respectively Taitle and Vixare, which can only be the Etruscan names for Daidalos and Ikaros. On another scarab he is named Taitle and flies over water holding saw and hammer. From the present scarab we might take it that the Etruscan artist thought wings appropriate to Daidalos quite apart from the story of the flight which proved disastrous for Ikaros, but on a ringstone he is shown, wingless, using an adze to finish a wing, so the Etruscans conceived the wings as wooden, and the act of carpentry shown here may not after all be unrelated to his aeronautics.

The man on *145* is in the grip of two snakes. They are not in his grip, so this is not the infant Herakles, nor are weapons shown, so this is not the grown Herakles with one of his ophidian adversaries. Since more than one snake is involved it is not likely to be any other hero who had dealings with single snakes, and since he is so enmeshed it is difficult to escape the conclusion that we have

43

Laocoon, or one of his sons in the coils of the serpents sent by Apollo. Since other scarabs with the three figures and snakes are of doubtful authenticity, the existence of this one, albeit with a single figure and of summary style, is of some importance for the early history of the iconography of the story.

Other myth figures are more straightforward. The swan-rider on *147* is seen on many scarabs and usually taken for Apollo's favourite, Hyakinthos, riding the god's swan. Herakles reappears with the stag, twice at the fountain, and resting (*148–151*). Satyrs are uncommon figures on scarabs but here there are two, one with his pipes and a goat, the other riding a dolphin and wielding a club (*153, 154*). Satyrs masquerade as Herakles on a number of Etruscan scarabs, including several on which the hero takes to the seas on a raft. But neither he nor a satyr take naturally to anything so intimately aquatic as dolphin-riding so this is another enigmatic scene, so far unique.

The carpenter on *157* adopts the pose and dress familiar from finer scarabs. The athlete, cavalier and chariot scenes, as on *158, 160, 161*, derive from the Archaic repertory, but the first seldom survive so late in this form. Other mortal activity with animals may involve sacrifice (*159*) or the hunt.

The remaining a globolo scarabs have the simpler beetle type with correspondingly summary intaglios. But there are still mythological subjects and some fantasy. On *170* Ajax falls upon the sword he has planted in the ground. Other and earlier scarabs give the figure in greater detail making the action explicit. The a globolo artist takes the elements of the picture only – man, sword, shield – and relies on the familiarity of the subject for identification. The ever-popular Herakles appears twice with the lion (*171, 172*). In this style, which rather lends itself to the rendering of knobbly clubs, we cannot be sure that all club-bearers are Herakles. When a bow is held also it may be clear (*173*) but the uprooted tree (*174*) is less obvious as an attribute or weapon for the hero. Satyr and winged man we have met before (*175, 176*). The former is remarkable mainly for the strictly Archaic pose of his legs and he reminds us how the Archaic beginnings of the scarab styles in Italy long dictated many subjects and poses, abandoned elsewhere in the Greek world.

The monster Skylla on *177* is understandably popular in the west. It is with the fourth century that she appears in other works with a frontal human torso attached to fishy tail and one or two dog foreparts, instead of in profile view. The weapons are various. Our figure is not obviously female and other Etruscan Skyllai on scarabs are simpler, even in this style. The monster on *178* is less readily named. Fishy figures are shown thus on scarabs – and called Tritons – but ours has a bird's claws, and we may be meant to take the three blobs as haunches and tail, a stylisation met for other plan views of monsters in this style. There are no wings, however, and this is no ordinary siren. Other monsters are conventional – Kerberos, a chimaera, sphinx, Pegasos and a griffin, representing the Classical form of the beast (compare *100* and the other a globolo version, *168*).

The relationship between man and animal on these stones is not always obvious. *186* might seem to show an acrobat, but if the man is holding a hammer (and possibly another implement in the other hand) he should perhaps be taken for a sculptor. The suckling foal certainly suggests something more static than a circus ring, but we cannot press details of this sort in this style: nor can we dismiss them as conventional since the suckling motif was not as commonplace in this period as it was in the Archaic, and was never as favoured in Etruria as it was in Greece and the east. On *188* it is possible that sacrifice is intended (compare *159*). Deer are sometimes shown harnessed in a chariot on these scarabs: on *189* one is ridden.

The interest in studies of craftsmen at work is a little odd, when one considers that these scarabs were probably intended for decorative use rather than sealing. An impression of *190* would make the carpenter left handed, and it is a general rule in this series to make the image right in intaglio, not in impression, while on earlier stones and on all Greek gems the reverse is true. This is why it is usually satisfactory to view these stones in original only. A number of the studies of men are puzzling or nondescript or entertaining – the acrobat on *193*. Animals are by far the commonest of the a globolo subjects, and among them we may pick out the popular frontal horses (*202*) and an odd displayed bird (*203*). Joined or split animal bodies were quite common Archaic motifs and they too are still found. Usually one head and neck is provided with two bodies. On *204*, two heads have one, spreadeagled body.

CHAPTER V

Eastern Seals

The east has been often mentioned in these pages, as inspiration for the Archaic Greek scarabs, as a home for Greek-inspired studios serving markets in the Persian Empire, as the source of motifs adapted and sometimes combined with Greek, for the western, Punic cities. Some purely eastern seals have been illustrated. Others, which are plentiful in this collection, must be ignored, and this brief epilogue is devoted to a few only, chosen to point the contrast with the Greek styles dominant on most of the gems shown in this book, or to illustrate the seals of that Syrian-Cypriot area out of which so much came to influence Greek styles and artists.

First, four haematite cylinders of Syrian type and Bronze Age date (*205–208*). A totally different world from the free animal art of Bronze Age Greece (*4, 5*); different too in its use or abuse of space, yet these repeated patterns of heads, deities and animals best suit the cylinder and looking at them we can see why the form never attracted Greek artists.

Haematite remains a characteristic material for seals in Syria in the early Iron Age and *209* is a precious example since it is preserved with its gold mount. In Syria and nearby Cyprus softer stones are also cut, often black or vari-coloured serpentines, and several of these pieces reached Greek lands. The scarab back is replaced by a negroid head on *210*, a common motif for these seals in Cyprus and derived from Egyptian seals, but the device is Levantine. In comparable style is another figure seal (*211*) with a more rare subject on the back – a lion cut in the round, its heavy head and square muzzle typical of north Syrian statuary of the eighth-seventh centuries: recall our Classical lion gem (*37*). In nearby Cilicia in the eighth century simple small scaraboids of soft stone were cut in a primitive style (yet not far removed from that of *209*) which draws on the same repertory of oriental motifs as the Syrian relief sculpture. The main merit of these pieces is the ease with which they can be recognised and the main interest their distribution through the Greek world and even to Etruria, for they were being made at just the time that Greek trade with the East and colonisation in the west were commencing in earnest, and in the hands of the same Greeks – from the Euboean cities. I show two of the examples in the collection, *212*, *213*.

The scaraboid *214* is of the period when the Archaic Greek artist was learning how to handle these harder stones. The subject is met often on Greek gems, but the creature attests none of the observation of anatomical detail which delighted a Greek artist, while the disc and crescent is a familiar eastern symbol which the Greeks did not copy.

Finally, a miniature work in the round (*215*: colour, p. 31), and from Egypt, which can hardly qualify for inclusion in a book devoted to gems except in so far as its material and size call for similar skills. It is the upper part of an Egyptian figure of Bes, probably of the late period when Greeks and Egyptians met more often, and when the Greeks could observe, in Egypt or the east, the likenesses between the grotesque Bes and their own satyrs.

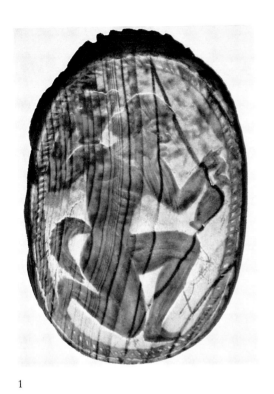

1   1

2   3   3

D

4

5

7

8

7

9

10

11

12

14

13

15

16

17   18   18

19   20   20

21   21

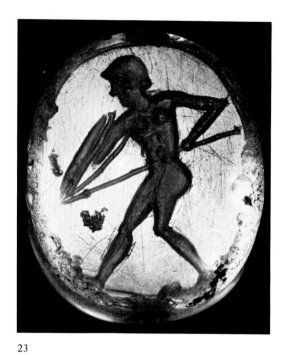

23

24

26

25

26

27

28

29

29

30

30

31

31

32

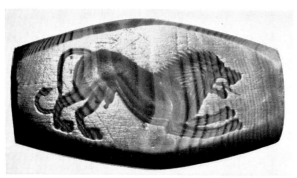

33

33

34

35

36

37

37

37

38

39

40

41

40

42

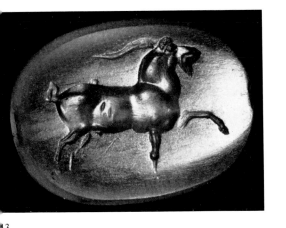

43

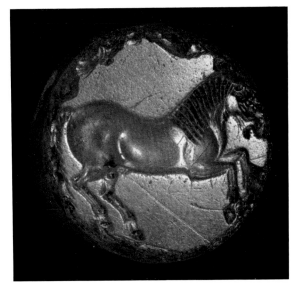

44

45

46

47

48

49

50

52

53

51

51

54

55

56   57   58

59

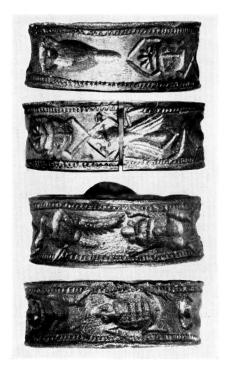

60

61

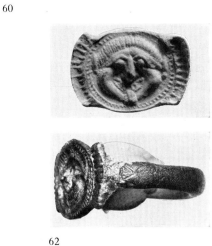

62

63

64

65

66   67

65

68

70

69

71

72

73

74

75

76

76

77

78

79

80

81

82

84

85

86

87

88

89

89

90

91

92

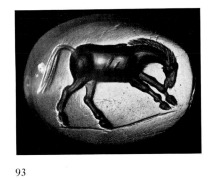

93

94

95

96

97

98

99

100

101

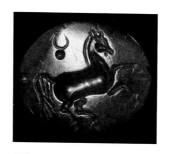

102

103

104

105

106

107

108

109

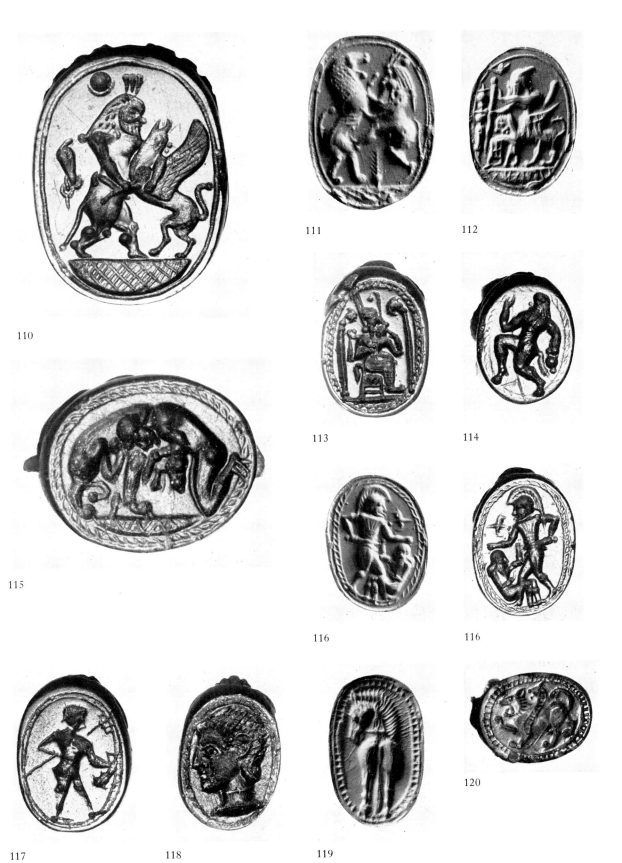

110

111

112

113

114

115

116

116

117

118

119

120

121

121

122

123

124

125

126

127

127

28

129

30

131

132

133

134

135

136

137

138

139

140

141

142

143

144

145

146

147

148

149

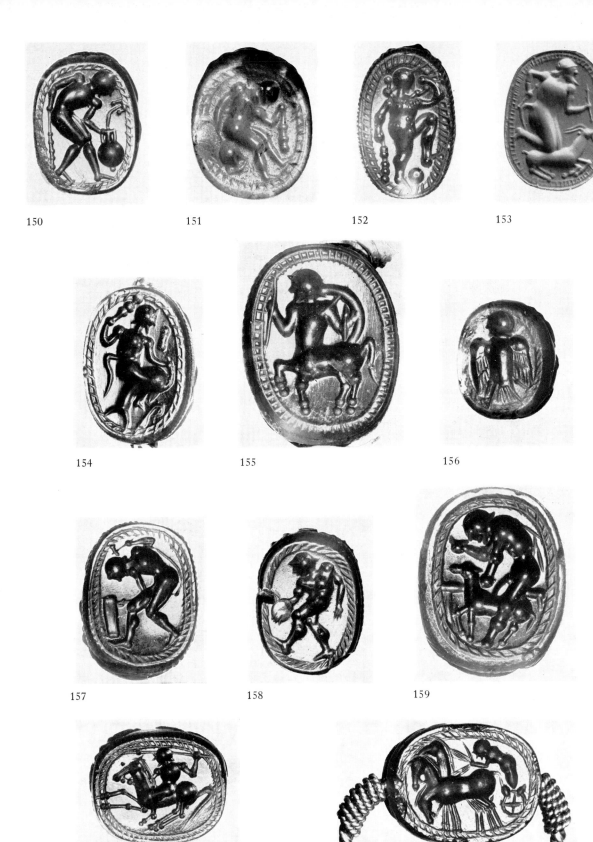

150

151

152

153

154

155

156

157

158

159

160

161

162

163

164

165

166

167

168

169

170

171

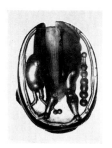

172

173

174

175

176

177

178

179

180

181

182

183

184

185

186

187

188   189   190   191   192

193   196

194   195

   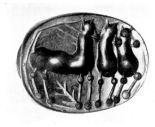

197   198   199   200

201   202   203   204

205

206

207

208

209

209

210

210

211

211

212

213

214

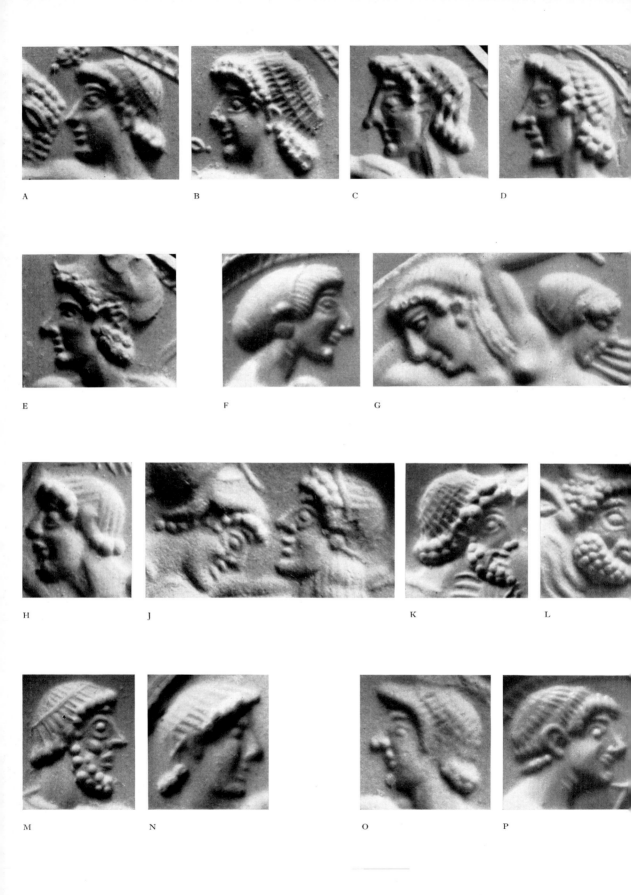

A   B   C   D

E   F   G

H   J   K   L

M   N   O   P

Catalogue and Notes

CATALOGUE AND NOTES

Measurements are given in millimetres. The first generally indicates the height or thickness of the stone, the second and third the dimensions of the engraved face. Descriptions refer to impressions but ambiguity is avoided.

(H) after descriptions indicates a hatched border to the intaglio, and for further abbreviations in Etruscan scarab descriptions see below. Greek scarab types are explained in *AGGems* 12-15 and scaraboids in *GGFR* 191f.

ABBREVIATIONS

AFRings	J. Boardman, 'Archaic Finger Rings' in *Antike Kunst* x (1967) 3-31
AG	A. Furtwängler, *Die antiken Gemmen* (1900)
AGGems	J. Boardman, *Archaic Greek Gems* (1968)
AJA	*American Journal of Archaeology*
BABesch	*Bulletin van de Vereeniging tot Bevordering der Kennis van de antieke Beschaving*
Berlin	E. Zwierlein, *Antike Gemmen in Deutschen Sammlungen*, ii, Berlin (1969)
ES	P. Zazoff, *Etruskische Skarabäen* (1968)
GGFR	J. Boardman, *Greek Gems and Finger Rings* (1970)
IGems	J. Boardman, *Island Gems* (1963)
JdI	*Jahrbuch des deutschen archäologischen Instituts*
JHS	*Journal of Hellenic Studies*
Kraay-Hirmer	C. M. Kraay and M. Hirmer, *Greek Coins* (1966)
London	H. B. Walters, *Catalogue of the Engraved Gems in the British Museum* (1926)
LondonR	F. H. Marshall, *Catalogue of the Finger Rings, Greek, Etruscan and Roman in the British Museum* (1907)
Munich	E. Brandt, *Antike Gemmen in Deutschen Sammlungen*, i, München, i (1968)

New York   G. M. A. Richter, *Catalogue of Engraved Gems, Metropolitan Museum of Art, New York* (1956)

Richter   G. M. A. Richter, *Engraved Gems of the Greeks, Etruscans and Romans* i (1968); ii (1971)

Southesk   Lady Helena Carnegie, *Catalogue of the Collection of Antiquities formed by James, Ninth Earl of Southesk* (1908)

GREEK GEMS

1 Chalcedony, blue-grey, patinated and lightly veined. Scarab with carefully cut head, legs and wings, bow-shaped thorax and v winglets. 12 × 20 × 14.' From Corinth'. *GGFR* 402, as *AGGems* 93bis.

A satyr kneeling, holding an amphora on his left shoulder, a jug in his outstretched right hand. (H)

By the Master of the London Satyr (*Burlington Magazine* 1969, 587ff.; *GGFR* 402). For the scarab back see *Burl.Mag.* figs. 15-17. Compare too the legs and belly markings of the satyr on the London scaraboid, *AGGems* pl. 9, no. 133 (*GGFR* pl. 312). The aggressive head and features resemble those of the satyr carrying off a girl on the fine Leningrad scarab (553: *GGFR* pl. 303) but the hand is different (leg and knee markings as others of the Slim Satyr Group).

About 530 BC.

2 Serpentine, pale green, partly translucent. Scarab, very roughly cut, with a large fan-shaped head, high thorax and angular mitre-shaped wing cases with ridge carination. 10 × 17 × 11. Once Abbé Nayem Collection.

A lion seated left on a short ground line, mouth open, tongue lolling. (H) By Onesimos. The scarab shape is exactly his (*AGGems* 119) and for the lion's body see the sphinx on a Paris scarab (ibid., pl. 25, no. 349; *GGFR* pl. 353). In *AGGems* he was assigned seven scarabs of this material, three of them signed. We should consider the addition of the amygdaloid in Athens with a contorted man-bull (*IGems* pl. 13, no. 350; *JHS* lxxxviii (1968) 1, (ii), pl. 1; *GGFR* pl. 273).

About 500 BC.

3 Cornelian. Scarab with simple back, incised legs, spine carination. 8 × 16 × 12. *Münzen und Medaillen, Auktion* xl (1969) pl. 1, no. 5; *Art of Ancient Italy* (Emmerich Gallery, 1970) 42, no. 65.

A gorgoneion, with snakes from hair and chin. Small human ears, no tusks or tongue showing. (H)

Related to the group represented by our *8*, where we find similar components – hair, eyes, snakes, jowls, but the whole form of the head has been re-styled.

About 500 BC.

4 Agate. Lentoid. 7 × 15 × 16.

A dog, twisting back to lick or sniff at a rear leg. Broad ground line.

Probably Minoan, Plain Palatial Style (*GGFR* 48). LM II-IIIA.

Late 15th to early 14th century BC.

5 Agate, reddish. Lentoid. 9 × 22 × 23. Part of the face broken away.
Three goats.
As the last.

6 Serpentine, pale green, partly translucent. Tabloid pierced lengthwise. 6 × 16 × 13.
A figure in long dress seated left on a folding stool. He seems to have long hair and
beard and some sort of headdress. He holds a stick in one hand, a branch in the other.
See *IGems* 82–4 and *JHS* lxxxviii (1968) 5f. for Island Gems not lentoids or amygda-
loids. Folding stools – see G. M. A. Richter, *Furniture of the Greeks, Etruscans and
Romans* figs. 236ff.
Early 6th century BC or earlier.

7 Cornelian. Scarab with a lumpy back and slight spine. 7 × 15 × 11. Set on a gold
swivel (W. 27) with globule terminals and in a hoop composed of beaded wire,
plaited wire, twisted wire and granule triangles, all on a sheet backing. Once Ephraim
Collection.
Bes fights a lion. Bes is naked but for a low headdress and the tail of the animal skin,
which is not otherwise shown. The lion claws his chest and leg, turning its head
away. (H).
Apparently a replica, with setting, of a piece from a tomb at Ialysos in Rhodes, with
pottery of about 520–510 BC: *Clara Rhodos* iii, 269, fig. 267.
Third quarter of the 6th century BC.

8 Cornelian. Scaraboid of Archaic form with high straight walls. 5 × 11 × 8. Set on a
gold wire-bound hoop with disc terminals, themselves fashioned as small lion masks.
A gorgoneion with snakes from hair, cheeks and chin. (H)
To be associated with the gorgoneion gems, *AGGems* nos. 66–69, and especially
nos. 66–68 (pl. 4) which may be by the same hand but are set differently on the
stone. No. 66 (*New York* no. 49, pl. 8) has an exactly similar arrangement of snakes
and compare our *3*.
Middle of the second half of the 6th century BC.

9 Cornelian, pale. Scaraboid of Archaic shape with high straight sides. 12 × 8 × 8.
A seated sphinx, one foreleg raised. Line border.
A plump, summary version of the creatures in the Sphinx and Youth Group I; cf.
AGGems pl. 9, no. 127, especially for head and paws.
Late sixth century BC.

10 Cornelian. Scarab with bow-shaped thorax, outlined elytra, a clear spine. 9 × 15 × 11.
A seated griffin, one foreleg raised. Line border, mainly broken away.
The heavily marked wing is as in Sphinx and Youth Group I, where there is a
scaraboid, in Munich, with the forepart of the monster (*AGGems* pl. 9, no. 130;
GGFR pl. 313) given a heavier, leonine mane. The slim-necked griffin, as ours, is
seen in the Flaccid and Summary styles (*AGGems* 135f.).
Late sixth century BC.

11 Agate. Scarab with a very worn back, simple legs. 8 × 12 × 9.
A man leading a horse. (H)
Summary version of the London scaraboid, *AGGems* pl. 10, no. 137, and cf. *GGFR*

pl. 349 (*Revue Archéologique* 1971, 202f., fig. 10).
Late sixth century BC.

12 Rock crystal. Scaraboid. 7 × 13 × 10.
Athena, standing left, wearing a helmet with low crest which leaves her face exposed, and a peplos. She holds a spear upright, point down, in her right hand, with her left hand on her hip. Line border.
Dry Style. Compare the London scarab (*AGGems* pl. 13, no. 207) where she again lacks her aegis but is carrying a shield and also wearing a himation. For this East Greek Athena type see Boardman, *Greek Emporio* 23, pl. 60. 785 (early sixth-century Chian plate); H. Herdejürgen, *Antike Kunst* xii (1969) 102ff., pl. 45.
About 500 BC.

13 Cornelian. Scarab with simple back, cut legs, spine carination. 10 × 19 × 14. A bald, bearded satyr, lacking a tail, carries in his arms a woman whose clothes and body are even more summarily indicated. Cross-hatched exergue and line border.
A very summary version of the Slim Satyr Group (*AGGems* 53ff.); for the subject see ibid., pl. 7, nos. 103, 104, 107 (the first also with a cross-hatched exergue, the last with a tailless satyr, but all satyrs with equine feet).
Late sixth century BC.

14 Cornelian. Scarab, rough with simple incised legs and gable carination. 8 × 13 × 10.
A siren standing over, presumably carrying, the body of a man. The features of both are only roughly represented and the man is armless. (H)
On a cornelian scarab from Chiusi (*AG* iii, 103, fig. 70; *AGGems* no. 168) a siren showing both wings carries a man who holds on with his arms (*not* the siren's arms, *pace* Furtwängler). The style is comparable (Sphinx and Youth Group II); ours perhaps rougher. For the motif on Etruscan and Punic gems see *AGGems* 76, n. 40; *Munich* ii, pl. 74, no. 654.
Last quarter of the sixth century BC.

15 Cornelian. Scaraboid with a high domed back and in·sloping walls, like Type C. 7 × 13 × 9. Set on a solid silver hoop (W. 24) with disc terminals, fastened with wire. From Tarentum.
Münzen und Medaillen, Auktion xl (1969) pl. 1.6; *GGFR* 402 as *AGGems* no. 127 bis. Eros flying holding a ribbon in his hands.
Compare the lumpily cut head of our *9*. Flying Eros in this pose is also represented in the Sphinx and Youth Group II (*AGGems* nos. 169–171) but the slim limbs and body markings recall the style of the finer Group I (*AGGems* pl. 9, nos. 126–7 for the head, no. 133 for the body). In the auction catalogue it is taken for West Greek work of *c*.480 BC.
Late sixth century BC.

16 Cornelian. Scarab with roughly cut legs but careful elytra, a hatched edge to the thorax and light spine. 10 × 16 × 10.5.
A kneeling youth plays the lyre (barbiton). (H)
Sphinx and Youth Group II. *AGGems* pl. 11, no. 162 for the hand, no. 163 for the pose (also pl. 9, no. 133).
Late sixth century BC.

17 Agate. Scaraboid of Archaic shape with high slightly bulging walls. $8 \times 13 \times 9$.
Herakles kneeling with bow in one hand, his club in the other. He has a short thick beard. The scratch on the surface in the position of an arrow is not original. Irregular hatched border.
Finer examples of this type are *AGGems* pl. 18, no. 269 and no. 270; on pl. 20, no. 301 he wears a lion skin (or at least the cap). In another common variant the club is raised. This is a pose popular on Phoenician and Punic stones where, as on some Greek, he is shown beardless. Here his beard is short. Dry Style, of good quality.
Late sixth century BC.

18 Cornelian with plain patches. Scarab with carefully marked legs (plain plinth), hatched bow-shaped edge to the thorax and a slight spine. $8 \times 13 \times 10$.
A youth stoops to scrape his right shin with a strigil. (H)
For the pose with both legs profile compare *AGGems* nos. 190, 310. Sphinx and Youth Group II.
Late sixth century BC.

19 Cornelian. Scaraboid. $6 \times 14.5 \times 11$.
A youth holding a shield stoops to pick up a helmet. Line border.
Dry Style. For the subject see *AGGems* nos. 260–1, pls. 17–8.
About 500 BC.

20 Cornelian. Scarab with careful back, small v at centre junction of elytra and thorax, and defined legs. $6 \times 12 \times 9$.
A youth holds a cock and lyre. (H)
For the subject see the Greco-Phoenician, *GGFR* pl. 416, and helmeted, pl. 325 (*AGGems* no. 178, pl. 12). Sphinx and Youth Group I.
Last quarter of the sixth century BC.

21 Rock crystal. Scaraboid, Type A, with upright walls. $9 \times 19 \times 15$.
A horseman. He is belted and the dress over his thighs is marked as a criss-cross. In the field the inscription *Moschos*. Line border.
The even strokes to the *mu* and the form of the *chi* do not much narrow the choice of home for the inscription. Rhodes, Euboea, the Western colonies are possibilities. The figure device was not designed to allow for the inscription which was added, possibly not in the artist's studio. Compare the manner of the Mandronax inscription on *GGFR* pl. 315.
About 500 BC.

22 Cornelian. Scarab with simple legs, hatched border to the thorax and ridge carination ending forward in a v. $8 \times 16 \times 11$. The background to the intaglio has been re-polished in recent times but the intaglio is intact.
A youth supports himself on a stick, held in his left hand which is cupped over its end while he adjusts the heel strap of the sandal on his right foot. The other foot is bare. (H)
By Epimenes, for whom see *AGGems* 92–4 with pl. 16, nos. 246–8 and *GGFR* 148 with pls. 355–7. For this pose *AGGems* nos. 216 (*New York* no. 35, pl. 6) and cf. no. 309, pl. 21 (one sandal, a boy helping), nos. 191, 192 (athletes; probably Etruscan);

and the Etruscan *ES* nos. 42, 43, pl. 13 (on the former, inscribed These=Theseus, the foot is not 'auf einem Felsen hochgestellt' but raised over the other, unoccupied sandal). One sandal – see M. Robertson, *Greek, Roman and Byzantine Studies* xiii (1972) 39ff.

About 500 BC.

23 Rock crystal. Scaraboid, Type A/C with shallow in-sloping walls. 10 × 18 × 15. From Tarentum.
Münzen und Medaillen Auktion xl (1969) pl. 1.4; *GGFR* 402, as *AGGems* no. 293 bis. A naked warrior striding forward with shield and spear.
Of the Group of the Tzivanopoulos Satyr (*AGGems* 104–6); compare the anatomy of the animal warrior, ibid., pl. 20, no. 293 (*GGFR* pl. 342). In the auction catalogue it is taken for West Greek work.
First half of the fifth century BC.

24 Cornelian. Scarab with simply cut legs, and ridge carination. 8 × 16 × 10.
A kneeling goat. (H)
Compare the Group of the Munich Protomes, *AGGems* 128–30, pl. 29, especially no. 407 (also *GGFR* pl. 324) by the Master of the London Satyr.
About 530–520 BC.

25 Cornelian. Scarab with hatched edge to the thorax, outlined elytra and plain legs. 9 × 16 × 12. Once Southesk Collection.
Southesk pl. 2, A34; *AG* pl. 9.57; Lippold, *Gemmen und Kameen* pl. 80.13; *AGGems* 135, no. 466 (wrongly assigned to the Flaccid Style).
A seated griffin, frontal, its head turned to one side and foreshortened. It is maned and the hook over its head is presumably part of a crest. Short ground line. (H)
Compare the more usual profile views, *GGFR* pls. 464, 465. An earlier frontal sphinx, *AGGems* pl. 13, no. 202. Late Archaic, good Common Style.
Early fifth century BC.

26 Cornelian. Scarab with plain legs and plinth but well cut elytra, a hatched border to the thorax with a v at the junction with the elytra and slightly pinched tail. 9 × 13 × 11.
A lioness, its neck turned back, head frontal, stretched over a suckling cub. The belly hair is shown, the mane is stippled. Two dugs are correctly placed. The muzzle may be deliberately foreshortened. (H)
Lionesses with cubs are a rare motif in Greek art. Compare two lionesses with cubs on gems by the Master of the London Satyr (*AGGems* nos. 411, 412, pl. 29) in an earlier style. A later, Greco-Persian version – *GGFR* pl. 959.
Early fifth century BC.

27 Cornelian. Scarab. The legs are simple, the back slightly carinated (pinched). 7 × 12 × 18.
Joined foreparts of a boar and a lion. Between the boar's legs an arrow-shaped plant or symbol. Crude hatched border.
A popular motif on Greek and Phoenician scarabs (*AGGems* 128 and n. 37). For the device between the boar's legs compare that on the Phoenician scarab with lions attacking a bull (*AGGems* pl. 27, no. 366) and our *28, 115*. Common Style.
Late sixth century BC.

28 Cornelian. Scarab with simple back and legs. Badly worn. $8 \times 13 \times 10$. Set on a gold ribbon hoop with disc terminals.

A lion attacks a ram. An uncertain device beneath the ram. The hatched border is mainly worn away.

A loose version of Scheme A for the lion attack (*AGGems* 123). Lion attacking ram: compare the Amasis Painter aryballos in New York, *Madrider Mitt.* xii (1971) pl. 29b. For the device below the ram see the last. Late Common Style.

Early fifth century BC.

29 Cornelian. Scarab with careful back, hatched border to the thorax and v at central junction of elytra and thorax. $10 \times 19 \times 14$.

Facing head of a lion, with two mice below. (H)

F. Willemsen in *Olympische Forschungen* iv, on lion head spouts. Lion and mouse fable, Babrius no. 107.

Second quarter of the fifth century BC.

30 Cornelian with clear patches. Scaraboid of Archaic form with high walls. $4 \times 10 \times 7$.

Head and neck of a woman. She wears a sakkos with her hair rolled over her forehead, and a necklace. Line border.

Compare the heads of whole figures as *GGFR* pls. 449–51.

About 480–470 BC.

31 Chalcedony, blue. Scaraboid, Type C. $16 \times 26 \times 23$. From an old collection in Tarentum.

A satyr approaches a sleeping maenad, his left hand outstretched, his right moving to draw back from her naked body the cloak on which she is lying, but which now covers only her lower thighs and legs. She rests on a low rock, her arms bent behind her head, which is frontal. Her hair is loose. Beside her a thyrsos.

Compare especially the style of *Berlin* pl. 35, no. 150 (*GGFR* pl. 546), ibid., pl. 549, and the finer pl. 482. For the subject on vases see Beazley in *Attic Vase Paintings in Boston* ii, 96–9, and for pictures H. Schaal, *Griechische Vasen in Frankfurter Privatbesitz* (1922) 19ff.

Late fifth century BC.

32 Jasper, yellow with red blotches. Scaraboid, Type A. $6 \times 13 \times 10$. From Turkey.

The upper half of a woman, naked, with the edge of a garment at her middle. Her head is thrown back.

Other objects alleged to be of this find are the gem *33*, fibulae (*Fig. 5*), five or six agate barrel beads (one measures 21×7), a plain scaraboid ($6 \times 18 \times 13.5$) of the same material as this but incorrectly pierced (twice from one end), and also in this stone a plano-convex rosette ($4 \times 12 \times 12.5$) also pierced across its face. The group could genuinely be from a single grave.

Last quarter of the fifth century BC.

33 Agate. Sliced barrel. $8 \times 18 \times 8$. From Turkey; see the last.

A crouching lioness.

For this shape see *GGFR* 199f., 409f., and pl. 520 (our *Fig. 7*) for the motif.

Third quarter of the fifth century BC.

34 Chalcedony, blue. Scaraboid, Type A. 8.5 × 20.5 × 17.

A youth leaps from a galloping horse. He holds a spear. (H)

For the motif on gems see *AGGems* 81; on coins of Himera, Kraay-Hirmer, fig. 66 (our *Fig. 2*). We would expect a lighter spear, not a heavy one with round butt, as here, but cavalrymen are shown with thrusting spears.

Second quarter of the fifth century BC.

35 Chalcedony, white. Scaraboid, Type A/C. 9 × 25 × 19.

A statue of Athena, frontal. Three uprights over the head suggest crest and raised cheek pieces. Locks of hair hang at either side. She holds shield and raised spear, and wears a long dress with peplos corners (?) hanging below her forearm, and zigzags beside the centre folds on the skirt. A base is suggested by a short ground line and one vertical.

For the subject compare *GGFR* pl. 599 (our *Fig. 9*).

Early fourth century BC.

36 Chalcedony, blue. Scaraboid, Type A. 10.5 × 27 × 21.

A woman rides a goose. She holds her dress over her head, like a sail, and is dressed. Coins of Kamarina, Kraay-Hirmer, figs. 150–1 (our *Fig. 3*). Bronze mirror, Züchner, *Griechische Klappspiegel* 5f., K51, pls. 1, 2. Nereids may hold their dress like this when riding sea creatures, and compare the *aurae velificantes sua veste*, statues in Rome (Pliny, *Nat. Hist.* xxxvi, 29), and the Aura on a vase of about 400 BC: A. D. Trendall in *Charites* (Festschrift Langlotz, 1957) 167–9. For Aphrodite on a swan, E. Simon, *Die Geburt der Aphrodite* (1959) 32–5.

Late fifth century BC.

37 Cornelian, burnt, with a cracked and discoloured surface. A lion gem, the back cut as a reclining lion with cross-cut mane and summarily cut feet. 8 × 20 × 10.

A youth standing left, left hand on hip, holding forward in his right hand something resembling a leaf. Before him a seated lion. Ground line.

For lion gems see *AGGems* 165f., *GGFR* 205, 412. Miss Maximova has argued in *Trudy Gos. Ermitazh* vi (1962) 122–33 (cf. *Numismatic Literature* lxxxviii, 22) that all are of the first half of the third century in date, but see *AGGems* 165f., no. 614, pl. 40 for a Late Archaic specimen. For the style of this figure compare *GGFR* pl. 584. He might be an Apollo or hero with a lion (which resembles a funeral monument!). There is a lion gem to be added to the list: Cabinet des Médailles (Chandon de Briailles Coll., dog and hare), and another in the same collection without intaglio. Another (Switzerland, private) from Cyprus, is mounted on a gold finger ring. Early Archaic lion gems – *IGems* 150f., 154f. and *JHS* lxxxviii (1968) 9–12 (ivory), *GGFR* pl. 219 (stone).

Fourth century BC.

38 Chalcedony, grey. Ringstone. Plaque with bevelled edges, not pierced. 3 × 15 × 11.

A woman seated on a chair, wearing sakkos, chiton and himation wrapped around hips and legs. She holds a mirror and appears to be adjusting her head-dress. Ground line.

Possibly cut down from a scaraboid since, from the style of the intaglio, this is unexpectedly early for a Greek ringstone of this flat shape.

Late fifth century BC.

39 Jasper, mottled red and yellow. Scaraboid, Type A. 9 × 19 × 16.

Artemis runs right, holding a long burning torch. Her hair is bound up, and she wears a short chiton, with long boots. Behind her the letters AΔ. Ground line.

A scaraboid in Boston marked AΔ, *GGFR* pl. 599 (our *Fig.* 9). Artemis, moving more slowly, with her torch upright and a dog beside her, but similarly dressed, appears on a fourth-century silver ring in London (*GGFR* pl. 764) and in this pose on a bronze ring in Munich (A2566, *Antike Kunst* xii (1969) pl. 33.6). Praxiteles in Antikyra: Pausanias x, 37, 1; Imhoof-Blumer and Gardner, *Ancient Coins* pl. Y, xvii. See G. Bruns, *Die Jägerin Artemis* (1929) 35, 50f., 62f. and cf. the Selinus sealings, *Notizie degli Scavi* 1883, pl. 6.83 (with dog) –86. Common Style. Fourth century BC.

40 Cornelian, mottled with white streaks. Scaraboid, Type A/B. 7 × 14 × 11.

A pigeon rising, carrying a rolled ribbon from a cord held in its beak.

Replica in Boston, *GGFR* 409, no. 88, where the bird is smaller on the face of the stone and less realistically posed. On carrier pigeons see d'Arcy Thompson, *Glossary of Greek Birds* (1895) 242. Rolled ribbons shown on the steps of a stele (R. M. Cook, *Greek Painted Pottery* pl. 50), on a painted stele (*JdI* xxiv, pl. 5) and in a stele crown (*AM* lxxix, Beil. 48.1). I am grateful to Donna Kurtz for these references.
Mid fifth century BC.

41 Rock crystal. Scaraboid with rounded profile, like Type C. 9 × 16 × 13.

A duck. (H)

An odd motif. The artist has done his best to indicate fluffy plumage and webbed feet.
Mid fifth century BC. (?)

42 Cornelian. Not pierced. A thick plaque with in-sloping walls, rough cut. Possibly a cut down scaraboid or a stone whose back was spoilt, and which was finished for use as a ringstone. 5 × 23 × 18.

A kneeling goat, its head turned back. Mane, rump and belly hair carefully marked, with deep folds at the neck and a zigzag lower edge to the neck hair. The hatched border is poor, perhaps not original although possibly supplied in antiquity for re-use of the stone (see above).

See *GGFR* 198 for discussion of animal gems of this style and period and compare the Archaic Fine Style beasts, *GGFR* pls. 394–7.
Mid fifth century BC.

43 Chalcedony, blue. Scaraboid, Type A. 7.5 × 16 × 11.

A goat walking, one foreleg raised.
Second half of the fifth century BC.

44 Chalcedony, blue. Round scaraboid, Type B. 9 × 16 × 15.

A horse running free.
Mid fifth century BC.

45 Chalcedony, grey. Scaraboid (back worn down for setting in a ring ?; not perforated). 7 × 20 × 16.

A bull walking. Ground line and line border.
Mid fifth century BC.

46 Chalcedony, blue. Scaraboid, Type C. 10 × 22 × 15.
A stag.
Compare coins of Kaulonia, *c.* 400 BC, Kraay-Hirmer, fig. 263.
Late fifth century BC.

47 Cornelian. Scaraboid, narrow, with very high wall and back, Type C. 7 × 14 × 8. Set on a solid gold hoop (W.22).
A plunging bull. Ground line and line border.
Late fifth – fourth century BC.

48 Jasper, black. Scaraboid, Type A/C. 10 × 27 × 20.
A plunging bull.
Late fifth century BC.

49 Chalcedony, blue. Scaraboid, Type A. 9 × 24 × 18.
A chimaera. The goat seems attached as an afterthought but the serpent-head tail (beardless) was intended. Ground line.
Compare the body, legs and mane of the lioness on a sliced barrel, our *Fig.* 7, *GGFR* pl. 520. Other Classical gems with a chimaera omit the goat's forelegs and the serpent tail, as *GGFR* pl. 577, where, however, flames do issue from the goat's mouth, as here.
Late fifth century BC.

50 Cornelian. Scarab with simply cut legs. 10 × 16 × 12. Set on a gold swivel with wire-bound ends and disc terminals, on a modern pin.
A lion is gnawing at the severed hind leg of an ungulate. Line border.
Contemporary Greek versions on a scaraboid in Péronne (*GGFR* pl. 619; *Revue Archéologique* 1971, 202f., fig. 12) where just the foot is shown, and on a lion gem in New York (*GGFR* 205, fig. 212). Compare too the Greco-Persian, ibid., 313, fig. 285; the far earlier treatment, *GGFR* 153, fig. 193; and the gold ring, A. de Ridder, *Coll. de Clercq* vii. 2 (1911) pl. 20.2870. The pinched body and three-quarter head indicate a date in the early fourth century BC.

51 Gold ring set with a blue chalcedony ringstone. Large hollow hoop with broad shoulders. The stone is not pierced and has a convex face. 22 × 15. From Tarentum. Once Ephraim Collection.
A stag standing. Ground line.
Fourth or early third century BC (the stone could be earlier than the ring).

52 Glass, blue. Scarab with long body. 8 × 16 × 12. Once Hirsch Collection.
Facing head of a woman.
For heads of exactly this type on pale green glass scaraboids see *GGFR* 416, nos. 429-31. Blue glass scarabs are rare, but found on some western sites.
Fifth century BC.

53 Glass, pale green. Scaraboid. 7 × 28 × 22.
Diomedes, kneeling with drawn sword and wearing a baldric for his scabbard, holds the Palladion, seen frontally, with raised spear arm and shield seen from the side. Short ground line. Line border.

A less well preserved specimen, apparently a replica, is *Munich* i, pl. 37, no. 325 (*GGFR* 416, no. 407). Diomedes is usually shown walking with the Palladion, and later leaping over an altar outside the walls of Troy (as *GGFR* pl. 1015).
Late fifth century BC.

54 Garnet, almandine. Ringstone with convex face and slightly concave back. 4.5 × 13 × 8.
A man lifts a child onto his shoulder.
For the flying-angel motif cf. the red figure vase, *ARV* 279, no. 7 (Boston).
Hellenistic. Second century BC.

55 Cornelian. Scaraboid, cut on its convex back, with half the stone broken away behind the string hole. 4 × 20 × 17.
Nike carries a trophy. She is naked but for dress around her legs. The trophy is composed of a Thracian helmet with raised cheek pieces, a corselet, a shield with centre boss and a long ribbon.
For the more spirited Early Roman version see M. L. Vollenweider, *Steinschneidekunst* pl. 37.6, and *BABesch* xliii, 74, fig. 11. For the type, A. J. Janssen, *Het antieke Tropaion* (1957) 129ff. Another early example on a silver emblema, *Kunstwerke der Antike* (Sammlung Käppeli) E4 (=K. Schefold, *Meisterwerke* no. 349).
Early Hellenistic. Late fourth – early third century BC.

56 Garnet, almandine. Ringstone with high convex face, flat back. 5 × 21 × 11.5.
A woman, naked but for a himation swathed around her legs and over her arm, rests her elbow on a column and holds a flower before her. Ground line.
Hellenistic. Third century BC.

57 Cornelian. Ringstone with convex face and flat back. 4 × 25 × 15.
Young Dionysos, naked but for a himation draped around his legs and forearm, stands with his elbow resting on a column, shouldering a ribboned thyrsos. A panther with raised forepaw stands by him. Ground line.
Cf. *Berlin* pl. 45, no. 215 (similar figure in slightly different pose).
Hellenistic. Third century BC.

58 Red clay impression from a convex ringstone. 15 × 36 × 30; the impression 28 × 20.
Eros stands frontal, a spear in one hand, a thunderbolt in the other.
Alcibiades' shield – Plutarch, *Alcibiades* 16.1; Athenaeus xii, 534e; and Pliny, *Nat. Hist.* xxxvi, 28 for a statue in Rome. A. B. Cook, *Zeus* ii, 1045–6 for the motif.
Late fourth century BC.

59 Garnet. Relief bust. H. 18.
Head of a woman, her hair rolled and bound in a fillet, drawn back to a bun, and largely covered by a veil.
Probably Berenike II, wife of Ptolemy III. She died *c*.222 BC.

The typology of ring shapes followed here is that of *GGFR* 157 (Archaic), 213 (Classical) and the Archaic rings are discussed in *Antike Kunst* x (1967) 3ff. (here *AFRings*) with addenda in *GGFR* 403f.

The Archaic silver rings are believed to be from Selinus in Sicily.

60 Silver. Type O, flat hoop. 19×6.
An amphora; a scarab beetle; a fly; a swan with raised wing and head to ground; a frog; a tortoise or turtle. (H)
Late sixth century BC.

61 Silver. Type O, flat hoop. 23×9.
A lioness facing a horse: a swan with raised wing facing a lioness with frontal head (not shown; the head is badly damaged by a crack). Only near legs are shown except for the hind legs of the horse and second lioness.
Compare the silver rings with a gold stud, *LondonR* pl. 26, no. 1025 and fig. 130 – lion facing boar, lion with frontal head facing rat (*AFRings* 27, O1; our *Fig. 11*).
Late sixth century BC.

62 Silver. Oval bezel. The solid hoop terminals are dotted snake heads holding the triangular member with a ribbed base which fits along the edge of the bezel (cf. Type E). 16×11; W. of hoop 22.
Gorgoneion. (H)
An unusual shape. Type E rings have ribbed ends to rectangular bezels as a rule. Some other early gorgoneion rings – H. Payne, *Perachora* i, pl. 79. 30, 35 (relief), bronze; *LondonR* no. 1024, silver; Sunium, *Arch. Eph.* 1917, 207, fig. 17 top left. Snake heads holding bezels – *Perachora* loc. cit.; *AFRings* J2, K4, M17. Other Archaic Western Greek rings – see *AFRings* 17 with n. 54, D8–10, F20–23, J3–4 (ribbed bars beside bezel, as here).
Late sixth century BC.

63 Silver. Type F, leaf-shaped bezel. The solid hoop has snake head terminals holding the bezel in their jaws. 18×10; W. of hoop 25.
A flying bird, one leg showing. (H)
Late sixth century BC.

64 Silver. Type F, long diamond-shaped bezel on a solid hoop, the ends brazed together. H. of bezel 7; W. of hoop 25.
A lion with head turned back. (H)
Late sixth century BC.

65 Silver. Type F, long diamond-shaped bezel on a solid hoop, the ends brazed together. A branch pattern (not tremolo) on the bezel sides. H. of bezel 7; W. of hoop 22.
A lobster. (H)
Late sixth century.

66 Silver. Type F, long diamond-shaped bezel on a solid hoop, the ends brazed together. H. of bezel 6; W. of hoop 22.

A spider; two leaves before it. (H)
Late sixth century BC.

67 Silver. Type F, long diamond-shaped bezel, on a solid hoop, the ends brazed together.
H. of bezel 6; W. of hoop 22.
A swan with raised wing, head to ground. (H)
Late sixth century BC.

68 Silver with a gold stud in the bezel. Type M, broad oval bezel with a beaded member
along the bezel edges as terminal to the solid hoop. 15 × 12; W. of hoop 22.
Pegasos with sickle wings, one lowered. (H)
Mid sixth century BC.

69 Silver, with two gold studs. Round bezel on a flat hoop, broken away. 10 × 10.
A seated sphinx with a foreleg raised and head turned back. It is doubtful whether
the creature is intended to be bearded. (H)
Mid sixth century BC.

70 Gold. Type I/II, flat leaf-shaped bezel with a slim, solid, stirrup-shaped hoop.
16 × 8; W. of hoop 20.
Nike flying, holding a flower and a branch (?). Rough hatched border.
Penelope Group: *GGFR* 215f., 417, especially nos. 465–7 with Nikai, of which the
last (ibid., pl. 658) resembles ours in having the decorated panel down the skirt, but
is otherwise finer.
Early fifth century BC.

71 Gold. Type III, flat leaf-shaped bezel on a solid stirrup-shaped hoop. 18 × 8; W. of
hoop 20.
A beardless youth (Herakles) reclining naked. Behind him stands his club and another
small object (? part of a quiver). In his right hand he holds out a cup – a kantharos
to judge from the relative positions of his hand and the bowl but the details here and
all round the edges of the bezel are badly worn (also removing his right foot).
Waterton Group, *GGFR* 216, 417. Compare the pose of Anakles' satyr with a cup
on the New York scaraboid, *GGFR* pl. 373. For the style compare the warrior on
the Boston ring, *GGFR* pl. 440.
First quarter of the fifth century BC.

72 Gold. Type M, flat leaf-shaped bezel on a slim solid hoop. 16 × 7.5.
Two birds flying with a snake between them. (H)
Late sixth century BC.

73 Gold. Type III, leaf-shaped bezel on a slim, stirrup-shaped hoop. 17 × 10; W. of
hoop 20. Once Ephraim Collection, from Tarentum.
A seated woman, her head bowed. She wears a belted chiton, the neck and sleeve
stitching clearly marked, and a veil (epiblema) with dotted edge over her head,
falling straight before her face and on her left thigh. She is seated on an object given
a separate flat base and rolled top, probably an Ionic capital, and holds a floral spray.
Ground line.
Comparable quality, the Penelope of *GGFR* pl. 687. For figures on Ionic capitals
(apparently not altars) compare a cornelian scarab in the Harari Collection (*Southesk*

A12, pl. 1; *AG* pl. 20.48; Lippold, *Gemmen und Kameen* pl. 25.6; boy, perhaps Apollo, with bird); a cornelian scarab once in Evans Collection (*Selection* pl. 6.97; winged woman holding a branch, mourning ?); *GGFR* pl. 758 (Tarentum; gold ring; winged woman kneeling). A near replica of the motif on our ring is in relief on a gold scarab in a Swiss private collection.
Late fifth century BC.

74 Gold. Type III, broad oval bezel, curved, on a slim ribbon hoop. 14 × 10.
A woman (Aphrodite) seated on a chair with splaying legs, her right arm hanging over its back, her left hand holding out a bird to which a small standing Eros stretches a hand. Her back hair is dressed in a sakkos and she wears a heavy necklet. Her chiton has slipped to bare her left breast and a himation is wrapped around her legs. Ground line.
The replica, without Eros, *GGFR* pl. 759 (our *Fig. 10*), and cf. 229, fig. 240.
About 400 BC.

75 Gold. Broad oval bezel on a slim ribbon hoop. 18 × 15; W. of hoop 21. Once Ephraim Collection.
A winged woman seated on a chair with splaying legs, her right arm hanging over its back, her left forearm resting on her thigh. Eros flies before her to crown her. She wears her hair rolled, an earring pendant, a belted chiton and himation wrapped around her legs. Ground line.
Compare the group, *GGFR* 227, fig. 239 and pls. 758, 760 (the first two from Tarentum) with winged women (discussed ibid., 285) of exactly this style. Probably to be added is *Southesk* i, pl. 11, L2 (*GGFR* 422, no. 720).
Late fifth century BC.

76 Gold. Thin leaf-shaped bezel on a flat open hoop with snake head terminals. 13 × 8; W. of hoop 19.
Herakles, beardless and naked but for a cloak wrapped around his left arm, leans on his club, holding an aryballos in his left hand and an uncertain object in his right, extended over a block altar with top and bottom mouldings. Ground line with short dashes beneath.
Compare the Herakles with Nike on *GGFR* pl. 769, and alone on *AG* pl. 61.31.
Fourth century BC.

77 Gold. Type IV, leaf-shaped bezel on a very thin hoop. 12 × 7; W. of hoop 18.
A bee. (H)
Mid fifth century BC.

78 Gold. Type XI, broad oval flat bezel on a heavy hoop decorated with three grooves. 21 × 19; W. of hoop 20.
A woman with a swan. She is naked but for a himation around her legs, her hair rolled with a lock escaping behind. She is seated on rocks, offering a dish to the swan, which bends its head to it, spreading its wings, and places its left foot on her knee.
For the scheme with Ganymede and the Eagle see Boardman, *Engraved Gems; the Ionides Collection* 33, 97f., no. 45. It is Ganymede, not Venus, on gems of the type,

Vollenweider, *Steinschneidekunst* pl. 96. 7–10; but Venus and the eagle, ibid., 82–4, pls. 1, 2, and seated on a rock with the eagle (not feeding it), pl. 96.3, 6. Bronze mirror from Eretria with Aphrodite riding on and feeding a swan: see above, on *36* and *Fig. 1*. Leda and Ganymede on sarcophagi: Robert, *Griechische Sarkophagreliefs* ii, pl. 2. 3, 4. Hygieia and snake intaglio: *GGFR* 233, fig. 261. Leda – E. R. Knauer in *Jb. der Berliner Museen* xi (1969) 5ff. She feeds the swan beside a tree with a bird on a nest on an Etruscan mirror, *Münzen und Medaillen Auktion* xxii, no. 81. Third century BC.

79 Gold. Round, slightly convex bezel. Thin hoop. 18 × 17; W. of hoop 20.
Erotostasia. A woman seated on a stool with heavy turned legs, holding scales in which she weighs erotes, only one shown clearly, the other obscured by her knee. She wears a belted chiton and himation around her legs, hair rolled and dressed to a topknot. Groove ground line filled with tremolo.
For the subject on earlier rings see *GGFR* 216 with pl. 666 and references on p. 296. Late fourth century BC.

80 Bronze. Oval bezel on a solid hoop. 15 × 10; W. of hoop 20.
Eros kneeling, holding an indistinct object (perhaps a iunx wheel) in his hands. Ground line.
Fourth century BC.

81 Gold. Oval bezel on a slim stirrup-shaped hoop. L. of bezel 17. From Sicily.
Two birds, a branch between them, standing on a laver, whose top and base are decorated with tremolo, a pillar between them. Branches at either side. Grooved border filled with tremolo.
For tremolo on gold rings see *GGFR* pls. 441, 687, 748, 751, 759, 760, 778–9, 784–5, 820–1. It is also used on two silver rings in this collection, not illustrated. On the technique, P. Jacobsthal, *Greek Pins* 209ff.; Boardman in *JHS* lxxxviii (1968) 12.

82 Silver. Type XI, oval bezel on a ribbon hoop. Part of the bezel badly corroded. 25 × 20.
Medusa head, with wings in her hair and snakes.
Fourth century BC.

GREEKS, PERSIANS AND PHOENICIANS

GRECO-PERSIAN

The writer has discussed the pyramidal stamps, as *83, 84, 86*, in *Iran* viii (1970) 21ff. and the scaraboids in *GGFR* ch. 6, in both places with full lists. For the Greco-Persian see also, recently, Richter, i, 125ff.; E. Zwierlein in *Berlin* 82f.; N. M. Nikulina in *Antike Kunst* xiv (1971) 90ff.
On hunting – J. K. Anderson, *Ancient Greek Horsemanship* (1961) especially 100–2. Xenophon on paradeisoi – *Anab.* i, 2.7 (at Kelainai in Phrygia); *Hist. Gr.* iv, 1.15 (near Daskylion); *Oec.* iv, 20 (in Sardis); on use of bow and javelin from horseback in hunting – *Cyr.* i, 3.14; and cf. *AJA* xvi (1912) 78f.

83 Chalcedony, white. Pyramidal stamp seal, not pierced through but for a pincer mount. 22 × 17 × 13.
A lion attacks a bull, collapsing forward with head turned back and back leg trailing. Very careful marking of all body detail. Ground line.
For the usual scheme see *Iran* viii (1970) 29; for the Greek, *AGGems* 123, Scheme A (and on Greco-Persian as *GGFR* pls. 867, 909, 935).
Late sixth century BC.

84 Chalcedony, blue. Pyramidal stamp seal, not pierced through but for a pincer mount. 21 × 15 × 12.
A monster which is basically a goat-sphinx with a boar's head and neck on its chest and its wing replaced by a lion seated, head back, forepaws waving. Ground line.
See *Iran* viii (1970) 35 with pl. 1, no. 8 (boar, goat-sphinx and horned lion heads, plus real wing) and 35, fig. 12, no. 161 for the boar as prey held by a monster in its forepaws, (these are our *Figs. 12, 13*).
Late sixth century BC.

85 Chalcedony, blue-grey. Cylinder. L. 26.
A royal hero holds two lions. Above, a winged sun disc. Behind him a linear device. Ground line.
For linear devices of this type see *Iran* viii (1970) 22ff. They are rare on cylinders (ibid., pl. 8, no. 198); for the dress, with bared forward leg, ibid., p. 31.
Late sixth – early fifth century BC.

86 Chalcedony, blue. Pyramidal stamp seal. 20 × 12 × 10. Once Abbé Nayem Collection.
A lion with raised forepaw. Cross-hatched mane. Ground line.
The combination of shape and motif: *Iran* viii (1970) 28, nos. 31, 32 (pl. 3, from Sardis), 140 (pl. 6), 141. The marking of belly hair is unusual in this style.
Late sixth century BC.

87 Chalcedony, blue. Scaraboid, Type C. 10 × 21 × 16.
A Persian, wearing the usual soft cap and tunic over a sleeved and trousered dress, rests his left hand on his hip, his right on the shoulder of a woman who holds a flower up to him in her left hand, a wreath in her right. She wears a loose-sleeved 'chiton' and wears her hair in a pigtail with three bobbles at the end. Ground line.
Arndt Group (*GGFR* 313f.). For the woman with flower and wreath, ibid,. 315, fig. 289; pls. 876 (bigger wreath), 879 (flower and branch), 880 (vase and cup); and the style of the man, pls. 876, 880. A whole group in this pose, pl. 891, or with the man holding a spear, 317, fig. 297.
Late fifth century BC.

88 Chalcedony, mottled grey-white. Scaraboid, Type A. 9 × 25 × 19.
A Persian dancing. Dressed as on the last, his hands clasped over his head.
Pendants Group (*GGFR* 316). For the posture see L. B. Lawler, *The Dance in Ancient Greece* 114f. with fig. 47; M. Emmanuel, *Essai sur l'Orchestique grecque* (1896) 210–8 (for pictures); L. Séchan, *La danse grecque antique* (1930) 173f.; B. Schweitzer in *Hermes* lxxi (1936) 288ff. On a gem, *GGFR* pl. 822. There is a Persian dancing with

krotala on a gold ring in a Swiss private collection (ring Type VI).
Late fifth century BC.

89 Chalcedony, blue. Tabloid. 11 × 14 × 19. Once Abbé Nayem Collection.
On the base – a Persian horseman draws a bow at a rearing lion. He is dressed as on
our *88*; the horse has a decorated saddle cloth and dressed tail. On the top – a
Maltese dog. On the shoulders – an antelope, a fox, a calf, a bear – all running.
Pendants Group (*GGFR* 316).
Late fifth – early fourth century BC.

90 Chalcedony, blue. Shallow scaraboid, Type B. 8 × 31 × 24.
Two birds pick at the prostrate body of a stag. Ground line.
Pendants Group (*GGFR* 316). On the antiquity of the motif in the Near East,
E. Porada in *VI. Internat. Congress of Iranian Art and Archaeology* 163ff.; on western
Anatolian pyramidal stamps, *Iran* viii (1970) 29; with a hellenised version, 27, fig. 6
(15). Compare the bird on *GGFR* 317, fig. 294; a prostrate stag torn by a dog,
fig. 296; a fallen deer, pl. 937; and a scaraboid in the best Greco-Persian style with a
single bird and a deer in the Wiegandt Collection (our *Fig. 14*).
Late fifth century BC.

91 Chalcedony, blue. Scaraboid, Type A. 9 × 24 × 19.
A crouching warrior, naked but for a pilos helmet, holding shield and spear. Ground
line.
Hellenising Greco-Persian. A near replica in Leningrad, *GGFR* pl. 954, and the
Greek version, once in Munich, *GGFR* pl. 534 (and compare 207, fig. 213, with a
different helmet).
Late fifth century BC.

92 Chalcedony, blue. Scaraboid, Type C. 9.5 × 25 × 19.
A seated hyena, striped. Ground line.
Other representations of hyenas on Greco-Persian gems are all small, on multifaced
tabloids, showing them running, crouching or walking, once wounded (*GGFR*
figs. 289, 290, 295 and 433ff., nos. 120, 124, 152, 226). Greek style of Greco-Persian
gems, as *GGFR* 311f.
Second half of the fifth century BC.

93 Chalcedony, blue. Scaraboid, Type A. 8 × 21 × 16.
A horse, nibbling or licking its fetlock. Ground line.
Group of the Leaping Lions (*GGFR* 317f.).
Late fifth century BC.

94 Chalcedony, mottled reddish grey. Scaraboid, Type A/C. 10 × 25 × 19.
A bull calf. Ground line.
Group of the Leaping Lions (*GGFR* 317f.).
Late fifth century BC.

95 Chalcedony, grey patinated. Scaraboid, Type A. 11 × 22 × 18.
A bull calf.
Wyndham Cook Group (*GGFR* 318).
Late fifth – early fourth century BC.

96 Rock crystal. Scaraboid, Type C. 11 × 20 × 15.
A quail. Short ground line.
Compare the bird on a scarab in Leningrad, *GGFR* pl. 902 (Pendants Group).
Second half of the fifth century BC.

97 Chalcedony, blue. Scaraboid, Type A/C. 11 × 32 × 33.
A lion attacks a stag.
Wyndham Cook Group.
Late fifth – early fourth century BC.

98 Chalcedony, blue. Scaraboid, Type A. 10 × 26 × 19.
A running griffin, head turned back. It has a horse's mane, a bull's tail and pizzle.
Ground line.
The mane is as on Court Style griffin monsters (*GGFR* pls. 838–41) rather than the
spiny Classical Greek mane seen on most Greco-Persian gems (as *GGFR* pls. 957–8
or our *100*) where the creature is normally winged. Close, however, is a stone once
in Berlin (*AG* pl. 12.45; *GGFR* 436, no. 302). Ibid., 432, no. 38 has a wingless
griffin, and the Oxus ring, 438, no. 403. The bull additives make this an odd creature
but the execution is as for the Greco-Persian Group of the Leaping Lions (*GGFR*
317f.).
Late fifth century BC.

99 Chalcedony, pale blue. Scaraboid, Type A. 10 × 26 × 19.
A leaping griffin, wingless.
Late fifth – early fourth century BC.

100 Chalcedony, blue. Scaraboid, Type B. 9 × 25 × 20.
A crouching griffin. Ground line.
Group of the Leaping Lions. Finer than most Greco-Persian griffins in this pose (cf.
GGFR pls. 957–8) yet lacking the fluidity of the more hellenised (*GGFR* pl. 868).
An unusual and Archaic feature is the forehead knob.
Mid fifth century BC.

101 Chalcedony, mottled brown. Scaraboid, Type A. 6 × 16 × 16. Set in a sheet gold
mount with a ridged loop handle and beaded wire at the circumference (total height
29). On the back a traced pattern of four outlined palmettes in a dot border.
A loose horse.
Bern Group (*GGFR* 320f.).
Late fourth century BC.

102 Chalcedony, grey. Scaraboid, Type C, with small perforation. 8 × 18 × 16.
A horse. A taurine symbol in the field.
Bern Group. Compare the horses on the name piece, *GGFR* pl. 965; and for the
device pls. 949, 984; and for the horn-like forelock, seen also on coins of Seleucus I,
p. 321. There is a near replica of this stone in the collection, without the device.
Late fourth – early third century BC.

103 Cornelian, pale. Scaraboid, Type A, not pierced. 6 × 22 × 19.
A horseman spears a boar.

Bern Group. Cf. *GGFR* pls. 973–5, with different quarry.
Late fourth – third century BC.

104 Agate, rosy. Scaraboid, Type A. 7×17×17.
Two elephants.
Related to the Bern Group.
Fourth – third century BC.

105 Rock crystal. Scaraboid, Type A. 6×16×15. Once Abbé Nayem Collection.
A lion attacks a donkey (?).
Related to the Bern Group. Compare the style of *GGFR* pl. 980.
Fourth – third century BC.

106 Chalcedony, blue. Scaraboid, Type C. 8×18×15. Once Abbé Nayem Collection.
A lion attacks a deer.
Bern Group. Cf. *GGFR* pl. 977.
Fourth century BC.

107 Chalcedony, greenish brown. Scaraboid with high in-sloping walls and a lightly
convex face. 10×17×14. Once Abbé Nayem Collection.
A reclining stag.
A globolo Group. Cf. *GGFR* pls. 981–2.
Fourth – third century BC.

108 Chalcedony, pink. Scaraboid, Type A. 7×16×15.
A reclining sphinx, with head-dress.
A globolo Group. Very close to the Bern Group; compare the head and head-dress
of *GGFR* pl. 966 and on the human-headed zebu on a gem of this group, ibid., 438,
no. 392.
Fourth – third century BC.

109 Cornelian. Scaraboid, Type A, with a slightly convex face. 10×21×18.
A running sphinx.
A globolo Group. Cf. *GGFR* pl. 988, which must be a sphinx also.
Fourth – third century BC.

GRECO-PHOENICIAN AND -PUNIC

Remarks on these gems by the writer in *GGFR* 153f., 403, *Bull. Mus. Hongrois*
xxxii–xxxiii (1969) 8–14 and *Revue Archéologique* 1971, 196–200. New publications
of the scarabs from Ibiza and Tharros are in hand as well as a general study of the
series.
For the Selinus sealings (terminal date 249 BC) see *Notizie degli Scavi* 1883, 473ff.,
especially pl. 12.153–65 for motifs as those on the scarabs.

110 Jasper, green. Scarab with deep cut legs and pinched tail. 9×16×12. Once Abbé
Nayem Collection.
Bes fights a griffin. Bes has a triple-feather head-dress, mane-like stippled hair, and

wears an animal skin knotted around his waist, the tail free. The griffin is crested. Above Bes a disc and crescent, behind him an upright uraeus cobra. Cross-hatched exergue. Line border.

Sixth – fifth century BC.

111 Jasper, green. Scarab, simple with hatched edge to thorax. $10 \times 15 \times 11$.
Bes fights a lion, the feather crown windswept. A branch below. Cross-hatched exergue. (H).
Sixth – fifth century BC.

112 Jasper, green. Scarab with simple back and very small elytra. $8 \times 13 \times 10$.
A king or deity, wearing a pointed cap and holding a sceptre, seated on a throne the sides of which take the form of an aproned sphinx. Before him a standed incense-burner (thymiaterion). Above, a rough disc and crescent. Cross-hatched exergue. Line border.
For this subject see W. Culican in *Australian Journal of Biblical Archaeology* i. 1 (1968) 57ff.; *Abr-Nahran* ii, 40ff.
Sixth – fifth century BC.

113 Jasper, green. Scarab with a pinched tail. 14×10.
Horus enthroned, his hand to his mouth. He wears the double crown of Egypt, shoulders flail and crook. Lotus columns at either side. Ground line. (H)
Sixth – fifth century BC.

114 Jasper, dark green. Scarab with pinched back. $6 \times 11 \times 8$.
A dancing satyr holding a jug. He has horse's feet. (H)
Compare *AGGems* pls. 6–7, especially nos. 84, 86, 102, noticing jugs and feet. Other representations of satyrs in the green jasper and related series are few: Leningrad 550 (squatting with goat and bow), Bibl. Nat. (Chandon de Briailles Coll.), *AG* pl. 15.18, 20 (cf. 17) and 7.30 (*London* no. 393). Cf. too the gold ring from Carthage, *Archeologia Viva* i. 2, pl. 14.
About 500 BC.

115 Jasper, dark green. Scarab with a pinched tail. $8 \times 13 \times 11$.
Herakles and the lion. Herakles is kneeling, legs together, throttling the lion whose jaws are gaping and who claws at his head with a rear paw. Beneath it a bud rises from the cross-hatched (broader one way) exergue. (H)
For similar poses on Greek vases of the 520's, *Jdl* lxxvi (1961) 49, fig. 1; 53, fig. 5, where Herakles' legs are not together, and he usually holds the lion's raised rear paw.
Early fifth century BC.

116 Jasper, dark green. Scarab, simple with a pinched tail. $6 \times 12 \times 9$.
A warrior with an old man. The warrior wears a Corinthian helmet and a corselet marked vertically and across the waist. He threatens with a sword and his left hand is clenched over the victim's head, as if holding his hair. The old man is bearded, apparently naked, raising his left arm in supplication, palm out, the other raised to hold the warrior's raised arm. Above him a trident sign. (H)
For the eastern scheme with a king or hunter and demon see W. Culican in *Abr-Nahran* ii, 42f.; on a scarab with Herakles and a small warrior, *Revue Archéologique*

1971, 196–8, fig. 4. A 'black agate' scarab, once in the Vanutelli Collection, 'from Greece', seems a near replica (*AG* pl. 9.16; Lippold, *Gemmen und Kameen* pl. 43.10), and there is another (whereabouts unknown to me) with an inverted T behind the warrior. Furtwängler took the former for Neoptolemos slaying Priam but it is probably another green jasper, hellenising an eastern scheme.
Early fifth century BC.

117 Jasper, dark green. Scarab, simple with pinched tail. 7×13×9.
A man holding a trident and a fish. Double line border.
Fifth century BC.

118 Jasper, dark green. Scarab, simple with pinched tail. 8×12×8.
Head and neck of a youth, with ringlets over the forehead and wearing a necklet. (H)
Fifth century BC.

119 Jasper, dark green. Scarab, simple. 8×13×9.
Back view of a horse. (H)
Compare the rear view of a horseman on a Greek gold ring, *AFRings* pl. 7, N43 and the scarab, *GGFR* pl. 311; and the green jasper scarab from Ibiza, Vives y Escudero, *La Necropoli de Ibiza* (1917) pl. 26.14.
Fifth century BC.

120 Serpentine, pale green, mottled. Scarab with long slim back. 5×10×7.
Chimaera. The goat's head is attached to a wing. (H)
Compare *London* nos. 382 (pl. 7), 414, 420 (from Tharros) and other examples in Sardinia for this group. The goat's head and wing scheme in Etruria – Zanco in *Studi Etruschi* xxxii (1964) 47ff.; Boardman, *Antike Kunst* x (1967) 9.

ETRUSCAN SCARABS

The following abbreviations are used in descriptions:
HT=hatched edge to thorax. VW=corner v winglets on elytra. OW 1, 2, 3 or 4= oblique corner winglets, single, double, treble or quadruple (these scarabs have plain plinths and simple legs unless otherwise stated). PL=plinth. PLH=hatched plinth. PLHE=plinth with hatched upper edge. (H)=hatched border to intaglio. (L)=line border to intaglio.

For an account of Etruscan scarabs see P. Zazoff, *Etruskische Scarabäen* (here *ES*) and for the early scarabs, idem, *JdI* lxxxi (1966) 63ff.; and *AGGems* 173ff., *GGFR* 152f.

121 Cornelian. Scarab with carefully cut back and legs, the head scalloped, hatched border to thorax, neatly feathered winglets, light spine, plain plinth. Set on a gold swivel made of two wires, twisted, and one straight, the terminals discs with lion masks. 7×12×9.
Mentioned by Zazoff in *JdI* lxxxi (1966) 72, n.21a.
Arming of Achilles. Achilles stoops to clip on a greave. He wears a Corinthian helmet and bronze corselet, the undergarment shown by loops over the thighs and

buttocks. Upright before him two spears with heads and butts clearly marked. Facing him is Hephaistos, bearded and apparently bare-headed (a cap may be worn), holding a shield with a flying bird blazon, wearing a knee-length chiton. His feet and toes are doubled back. Behind him is Thetis, in chiton and himation, with a head scarf, raising one hand in greeting. Line and dots border. Cross-hatched exergue.

By the Master of the Boston Dionysos, for whom see Zazoff in *JdI* lxxxi (1966) 63ff. and *ES* 17ff.; *GGFR* 153. His works are: 1. Boston 21.197 from Rome. Pseudo-scarab with Herakles fighting Nereus or Geras (?); Dionysos in relief on the back. Beazley, *Lewes House Gems* pls. 2, 8, 9, no. 35ter; *JdI* lxxxi (1966) 69, fig. 4 and *ES* pl. 7, no. 18; *AGGems* pls. 5, 38, no. 77; *GGFR* pl. 408; M. L. Vollenweider, *Die Porträtgemmen der romischen Republik* (1972) pl. 1.1. Our *Fig. 15*. 2. Our *121*. Arming of Achilles. 3. Vatican, Mus. Etr. Greg. 13.174 from Vulci. Arming of Achilles. *JdI* lxxxi (1966) 65, fig. 3; *ES* pl. 5, no. 17. 4. Florence 15260. Warrior (Achilles). *JdI* lxxxi (1966) 65, fig. 2; *ES* pl. 6, no. 16; Vollenweider, op. cit., pl. 1.2. 5. Oxford F74 from Corneto. Youth. *JdI* lxxxi (1966) 65, fig. 1; *ES* pl. 6, no. 15; *GGFR* pl. 409. 6. Paris, Louvre Bj. 1193. Woman. *GGFR* pl. 410. 7. Rome, Villa Giulia. Youth (clothed). Vollenweider, op. cit., pl. 1.3.

Related most closely are the Athenas on scarabs in Leningrad (667, *AG* pl. 16.11; Richter, i, no. 739; our *Fig. 17*) and Geneva (*Cat. Genéve* i, pl. 85, no. 221) and Dionysos on *AG* pl. 16.16 (Corneto).

Hephaistos' feet, cf. Corinthian (*JHS* lxxxv (1965) pl. 24) and Caeretan (C. M. Robertson, *Greek Painting* 77); V. K. Lambrinoudakis, *Merotraphes* (1971) 32ff., pl. 3. For Thetis with Hephaistos on Athenian vases of the 480's, K. F. Johansen, *The Iliad in Early Greek Art* 178–84; and B. K. Braswell in *Classical Quarterly* 1971, 19ff. for their special association in Homer.

About 520–510 BC.

122 Cornelian. Scarab with carefully cut legs but plain plinth, winglets, a hatched edge to the thorax with a small semi-circle at the centre. 7×12×10.
A dancing satyr with equine feet. Dot border.
About 500 BC.

123 Cornelian, patinated white through burning. Scarab. HT: PLHE. 6×11×8.5.
A naked youth stoops to scrape his right leg with a strigil. (H)
Cf. the Greek scaraboid once in Oxford, *AGGems* no. 259, pl. 17.
About 500 BC.

124 Agate. Scarab with traces of winglets. HT: PLHE. 9×14×10. Once Bale and Southesk Collections.
AG pl. 20.1; *Southesk* i, pl. 1, A10; *ES* no. 847.
A collapsing warrior holding a shield. His helmet (Corinthian) falls behind him. (H) The kneeling pose with shield – *ES* nos. 79, 80, pl. 20, and for a fallen helmet, no. 82, pl. 21 and *New York* no. 166, pl. 28 (*ES* no. 843): *ES* nos. 79 and 82 are inscribed Tute=Tydeus, and the New York scarab shows Kapaneus (with bolt). For the hand see *ES* no. 62, pl. 18 (with falling sword) and *Revue Archéologique* 1971, 205, fig. 15 (Péronne). On falling helmets, Beazley, *Attic Vase Paintings in Boston* ii, 20f.

125 Cornelian. Scarab with well cut legs, plain plinth, winglets, HT. 6×11×9.

A winged woman in a long dress holds a flower. A bird is perched on one wing. (H)
Mid fifth century BC.

126 Cornelian. Scarab. HT: VW: PLH. 7 × 13 × 10.
A winged woman in long dress. (H)
Fifth century BC.

127 Cornelian. Scarab. HT: VW. The plinth is herring-bone hatched. 8 × 15 × 12.
A warrior and youth. The youth, with a himation around his waist, sits on a rock
clasping one knee in both hands. The warrior stands, wearing leather corselet,
holding shield and helmet (Chalcidian). (H)
By the same hand on a similar beetle, *ES* no. 89, pl. 22 and cf. the satyr of Bibl. Nat.
N4121.
Second half of the fifth century BC.

128 Cornelian. Scarab. HT: VW: PL – cross-hatched. 10 × 16 × 12.
A winged youth holding spear and shield, a chlamys draped over his arms. (H)
On these subjects *ES* 96. Compare especially *ES* no. 420 (*London* no. 659, pl. 11)
and for the style nos. 151–2, pl. 31.
Late fifth century BC.

129 Cornelian. Scarab with worn back. PL – alternate hatching. 8 × 15 × 11.5.
A man stoops with outstretched hands towards a line of waves with a stippled area
(beach) above them. He wears a chlamys at his back. (H)
For the motif *ES* nos. 137 (our *Fig. 18*), 138, pl. 29 (*Munich* ii, no. 712, pl. 82) and
a scarab in private possession in Gloucestershire (perhaps not ancient). The Taitle
on *ES* no. 1333 (*AG* pl. 64.27) should not be read as Tantalos; see on our *146*.
Late fifth century BC.

130 Cornelian. Scarab. HT: VW: PLH. 8.5 × 14 × 11.
Münzen und Medaillen Auktion xl (1969) pl. 1, no. 8; *Art of Ancient Italy* (Emmerich
Gallery, 1970) 21, no. 27.
A young man wearing himation and chiton, and holding a shield and a wheel, starts
forward. Behind his head a star. (H)
See the publications cited for the explanation as Pelops. For the urns, Brunn-Körte,
Rilievi delle Urne Etrusche ii (1890) pls. 41, 45, 47, where the dress is different and the
wheel is used as a weapon. Scarab with winged woman with spear and wheel: *Kultura
i Iskusstvo Etrurii* (Leningrad, 1972) no. 235.

131 Cornelian. Scarab. HT: PLH. 9 × 15 × 12.
A youth stoops to lift three slim objects from the narrow neck of a round pot. His
left foot rests on a stone, behind his right is a long flat object with bevelled end. (H)
Late fifth century BC.

132 Cornelian. Scarab. HT: plinth not visible. Modern setting (compare our *184* and *AA*
1970, 157, figs. 1–5, as of Napoleon III period). 7 × 15 × 10.
A youth stands at an altar, placing round objects upon it, supporting himself on a
staff. He wears a chlamys at his back. The altar is a block with two cross pieces above.
The youth's left foot seems oddly braced against a wedge-shaped object beside the
altar. (H)
Compare the altar and objects beside the Herakles on *ES* no. 181, pl. 36, and *New*

York no. 213, pl. 33 (*ES* no. 1143) where the objects are clearly fruit.
Late fifth century BC.

133 Cornelian. Scarab. HT: VW. 7×15×11. Set on a gold swivel with lion masks on the terminals.
A naked archer, kneeling. (H)
Late fifth century BC.

134 Cornelian. Scarab. HT: PLH. 9×15×10.
A young man, shield on arm, is holding a helmet. Before him a sword in its scabbard. (H)
Cf. *ES* nos. 58, 59, pl. 17, for earlier versions, with the helmet and sword laid aside; and nearer ours in date, *AG* pls. 16.56, 62 and 20.7. A Greek version, our *19*.
Second half of the fifth century BC.

135 Cornelian. Scarab. HT: VW: PLHE. 15×12.
A man fastens a boot, wearing the other. His chlamys flies free behind him. His foot is raised on two flat steps. Behind him a shield. (H)
Early fourth century BC.

136 Cornelian. Scarab with simple back and legs. 8×12×10.
A satyr stoops over a calyx crater. (H)
Cf. the a globolo treatment of the subject, *AG* pl. 19.17.

137 Cornelian. HT: VW: PLH. 8×17×13.
A naked man seated on a folding stool hammers a roughly square object on an upright anvil. He wears a cap or head cloth. Ground line. (H)
Fourth century BC.

138 Cornelian. Scarab. HT: VW: PLH. 7×12×8.
Herakles lifts a rock. He is beardless, naked but for his lionskin of which we see a leg and tail. (H)
Herakles throws a boulder into water (the Strymon?) on *AG* pl. 18.17 (*ES* no. 609) where, however, the water is shown; and W. Martini, *Die Etruskische Ringsteinglyptik* (1971) pl. 2.4–5.

139 Cornelian. Scarab. HT: VW: PLH. 7×13×10.
Herakles at a fountain. He holds club and pot. The fountain has a lionhead spout. (H)
For subject and pose cf. *ES* nos. 66–7, pl. 18.

140 Onyx. Scarab. VW: PLHE. 7×12×9. Once Hamilton-Gray and Southesk Collections.
Southesk i, pl. 1, A5.
Herakles with the Stymphalian Birds. He holds a club in one hand, one of the birds by its neck in the other, and tramples another bird underfoot (taken for a trap in the Southesk publication). (H)
Early fourth century BC.

141 Cornelian. Scarab with oblique corner winglets, the feathers roughly marked. PLHE. 9×14×11. Set on a gold hoop of twisted wire with lion-head terminals.
Kapaneus. He is upright, falling back, his hair streaming, holding sword and shield.

H   105

Between his legs the thunderbolt, and before him rocks or the ladder (?). Inscribed AVO. Border worn away.

For the hair cf. the 'Tydeus' of *ES* no. 82, pl. 21. There could be confusion here with figures of Ajax thrusting the sword into his side, or the alternative suicide scheme with the ground shown as here (see *Antike Kunst* xvi (1973) pl. 9.4, 5, for the types on Etruscan scarabs).

Fourth century BC.

142 Jasper, black. Scarab with large corner winglets of diamond shape and ridge carination. HT: PLHE. 8 × 11 × 8.
Helmeted head. (H)
Fourth – third century BC.

143 Cornelian. Scarab. HT: VW: PLH. 8 × 16 × 12. The intaglio is chipped at one side. Once Evans Collection.
A helmeted head, the helmet (Corinthian) pushed back. (H)
Third – second century BC.

144 Cornelian. Scarab with heavy zigzag edge to head. HT: VW: PL – double hatched. 11 × 20 × 15. Once Festa Collection.
Eros crowns Athena (?). The goddess seems to be bare-headed, wears a long dress and holds shield and spear, with one arm behind the figure of Eros flying up before her, hands outstretched. (H)
An Eros crowning Herakles, *ES* no. 183, pl. 36.
Fourth century BC.

145 Cornelian. Scarab. HT: VW: PLH. 8 × 15 × 11.
A man collapsing, attacked by two snakes. (H)
For Laocoon on scarabs see M. Maaskant-Kleibrink, *BABesch* xlvii (1972) 135ff.

146 Cornelian. Scarab. HT: VW: PLHE. 8 × 15 × 12.
A winged carpenter. A naked winged man hacks at a flat board with an adze. (H)
Daidalos with adze and saw, *London* no. 727, pl. 12, *ES* no. 184, pl. 36 (as Eros; Richter, i, no. 863, as Daidalos; our *Fig. 19*). Winged Daidalos with tools on *London* no. 663, pl. 11 (saw and hammer; over water; inscribed Taitle; Richter, i, no. 862); no. 728, pl. 12 (*ES* nos. 397, 399); working on a wing on the ringstone in Péronne, *Revue Archéologique* 1971, 212f., fig. 29. The Baltimore bulla – G. M. A. Hanfmann, *AJA* xxxix (1935) 189ff. The inscription Taitle on *ES* no. 1333 (*AG* pl. 64.27) cannot be translated Tantalos but need not indicate a Daidalos.

147 Cornelian. Scarab. HT: VW: PLH. 10 × 17 × 13.
Hyakinthos rides the swan. He holds a goad; the swan is harnessed. (H)

148 Cornelian. Scarab. HT: VW: PLHE. 7 × 14.5 × 11.
Herakles and the stag. He is naked, holding a club in one hand, the creature's neck or horn with the other. (H)
A common motif on scarabs; cf. *ES* no. 263, pl. 50; *AG* pl. 19.5 (=*ES* no. 618, very similar to ours); *Berlin* no. 264, pl. 54 (=*ES* no. 620).

149 Cornelian. Scarab. HT: VW: PLH. 9 × 15 × 12.
Herakles with bow and club before a lion-head fountain. (H)

150 Cornelian. Scarab with finely detailed winglets. HT. 8 × 13 × 10.
Herakles with a club, filling an amphora at a lion-head fountain. (H)

151 Cornelian, opaque rosy. Scarab. VW: PLH. 8 × 13 × 11.
Herakles seated on an amphora, holding his club, head bowed. (H)

152 Cornelian. Scarab. HT: VW: PLH. 7 × 15 × 9.
Herakles stands, one leg raised, holding a club. His other hand is raised to his head. The devices over his shoulders might be part of the lionskin, but this is far from certain. A blob below. (H)

153 Cornelian. Scarab with detailed winglets with a hook rising from them. HT: PLHE. 8 × 14 × 10.
A satyr holding pipes kneeling over a goat. (H)
For the scarab winglets and hook cf. *ES* no. 2, pl. 2. A satyr kneeling over a goat on Liverpool 56.28.387. Satyrs imitating Herakles in this pose with the deer, *ES* nos. 630–3.

154 Cornelian. Scarab. HT: VW: PLHE. 9 × 14 × 11.
A satyr holding a club or branch, riding a dolphin, holding its muzzle. A long blob before him; a wave beneath. (H)
Compare the 'Phalanthos' on a dolphin on Tarentine coins and some scarabs, *ES* 134 and nos. 1190–1.

155 Cornelian. Scarab. HT: VW: PLHE. 10 × 19 × 14.
A centaur with shield and spear. (H)

156 Cornelian. Scarab. HT: VW. 7 × 11 × 9.
A siren displayed, legs spread, head turned. (H)
Similar is D. Osborne, *Engraved Gems* (1912) pl. 13.17 (but displayed across the stone).

157 Cornelian. Scarab HT: PLH. 9 × 14 × 11.
A man stoops to work at a block (anvil ?) with a hammer. He wears a chlamys. (H)

158 Cornelian. Scarab. HT: VW: PLHE. 8.5 × 13 × 10.
A man holding a discus. (H)

159 Cornelian. Scarab HT: VW: PL – alternate hatched. 11 × 17 × 14.
A man wearing a chlamys at his back kneels over the back of an animal, perhaps a calf, before a T-shaped altar. His raised hand holds what seems to be a cup but might be intended for a knife – for sacrifice. (H)

160 Cornelian. Scarab with winglets. PLHE. 8 × 14 × 12.
A horseman with spear poised. (H)

161 Cornelian. Scarab with finely detailed winglets. HT. 8 × 15 × 11.5.
A man in a three-horse chariot. (H)

162 Cornelian. Scarab. HT: VW: PL – cross hatched. 7 × 13 × 10.5.
A man holding a cleaver, with a dog before him. (H)

163 Cornelian. Scarab. HT: VW: PLH. 10 × 17 × 13.
A hunter with a curved throwing stick holds a stag by its horns. (H)
Compare the scheme of the satyr with a stag, *ES* no. 165, pl. 33, in this style.

164 Cornelian. Scarab. HT: VW: PLHE. 7.5 × 14 × 11. Set on a gold hoop of twisted wire
with lion head terminals.
A man fastens a sandal. His chlamys flies behind him. Behind his back a shield below
the end of a spear (?). (H)

165 Cornelian. Scarab. HT: VW: PLHE. 7 × 13 × 10.
A kneeling man (one thigh shown frontal) holding a staff or spear and a small pear-
shaped object in the other hand. (H)

166 Cornelian. Scarab. HT: VW. 7.5 × 14 × 11.
A warrior with sword and shield, stooping. (H)

167 Cornelian. Scarab with detailed winglets. HT. 7 × 13 × 10.
A warrior with helmet, shield and reversed spear. (H)

168 Cornelian. Scarab with roughly incised winglets. HT. 5 × 12 × 9.
A crouching griffin with short, bristling mane and long hooked beak. (H)

169 Cornelian. Scarab. HT: VW: PLH. 8 × 15 × 11.
A lioness with facing head, raised forepaw, dugs along the belly. (H)
For subject and style compare the chimaera, *Berlin* no. 276, pl. 55.

170 Cornelian. Scarab. HT. 9 × 12 × 10.
Ajax stoops towards his sword. A shield before him. (H)
A fuller version of this scheme is *ES* no. 145, pl. 30.

171 Cornelian. Scarab. OW3. 6 × 15 × 10.
Herakles and the lion. The creature's head is tucked under his arm. His bow is
behind him. (L)

172 Cornelian. Scarab. OW3. 7 × 14 × 10.
Herakles and the lion. The centre part is broken away. The creature is upright,
facing the hero, no doubt with its head held beneath his arm. Behind Herakles his
club. (L)

173 Cornelian. Scarab. OW3. 9 × 14 × 11.
Herakles with club and bow.

174 Cornelian. Scarab. OW3. 6 × 16 × 10.
A man stands holding a club and an uprooted tree. (L)

175 Cornelian. Scarab. OW2. 7 × 15 × 10.
A satyr playing double pipes. His near leg is turned frontal. There are cross pieces
near the mouths of the pipes, perhaps indicating flaring ends. (L)

176 Agate. Scarab with plain back and plinth. $7 \times 13 \times 10$.
A winged figure kneeling, holding a knobbed stick. (H)

177 Cornelian. Scarab. ow4. $7 \times 13 \times 10$.
Skylla (?) A human forepart holding a spear and two dog foreparts with one foreleg shown attached to a plump fishy body with fins and a short forked tail. (L)
Constructed with a single dog forepart and holding a sword on *ES* no. 172, pl. 35. The single animal forepart is normal on Greek gems (*GGFR* pl. 453 and p. 287) and finger rings (*Papers of the British School at Rome* xxxiv (1966) 7 and pl. 2, no. 15). See also A. Rumpf, *Die Meerwesen* (Ant. Sarkophagreliefs v.i, 1939) 107.

178 Cornelian. Scarab. ow3. $6.5 \times 13 \times 10$.
A siren (?). Human upper part seen frontal, holding two sticks raised, attached to a three-lobed body with spread claws. (L)
For the demon with clubs as Triton (?) with animal foreparts as legs see *ES* no. 255, pl. 48, and nos. 1563–5. *London* no. 870 (=*LondonR* no. 324) is a replica, but the figure has hands on hips and the claw feet are omitted.

179 Cornelian. Scarab. ow3. $6 \times 12 \times 9$.
A centaur holding an animal's head (? bull). Another head below his body. (L)

180 Cornelian. Scarab. ow3. $6 \times 11 \times 8$.
A centaur holding a club or branch.

181 Cornelian. Scarab. ow3. $6 \times 11 \times 9$.
Kerberos. Three dog heads raised, one of them turned back. (L)

182 Agate. Scarab with plain back and plinth. $6 \times 10 \times 8$.
A chimaera. The serpent head on the tail is not shown. (H)

183 Cornelian. HT: ow2. $8 \times 15 \times 11$.
A sphinx-chimaera. Human head, goat's (?) neck and head at the back, dugs along the belly. (H)

184 Cornelian. Scarab. ow2. $6 \times 13 \times 9$. For the setting see also *132*. Once Furtwängler Collection.
Pegasos. Two blobs below the body suggesting rocks. (L)

185 Cornelian. Scarab, the back cut down. $5 \times 14 \times 9$.
A crouching griffin with one foreleg raised. (L)

186 Cornelian, patinated white. Scarab. ow2. $9 \times 16 \times 13$.
A man standing on a horse's back holding its rein (?) and in his other hand a hammer. Below, a foal. (L)
Compare the man kneeling on a horse's back, *ES* no. 275, pl. 51 and no. 1236, and our *153*.

187 Cornelian. Scarab with plain back and plinth. $8 \times 13 \times 10$.
A man riding a horse (?). (H)

188 Cornelian. Scarab. ow2. $8 \times 15 \times 11$.
A man holding a spear kneels over the back of an animal (a deer ?). (L)

189 Cornelian. Scarab. ow3: PL – oblique hatched. $7 \times 13 \times 10$.
A man riding a stag. (H)
A man rides one of three stags on *ES* no. 476 (Rome, Mus. Naz. 69663).

190 Cornelian. Scarab. HT. ow2. $6 \times 13 \times 10$.
A carpenter. He sits on a block working at a stick with an adze, his cap hanging at the back of his neck. (H)

191 Cornelian. Scarab. HT: ow1. 14×11.
A man stoops to pick up a stick from which a forked object is hung. (H)

192 Cornelian. Scarab. ow2. $7 \times 15 \times 11$.
A man holding a sword. A blob and two bars in the field. (H)

193 Cornelian. Scarab with high plain plinth. HT: ow3. $7 \times 12 \times 9$.
An acrobat performing a somersault. (H)
Style and subject as *ES* no. 272, pl. 51.

194 Cornelian. Scarab. ow4. $10 \times 13 \times 13$.
A lion with an animal head between its paws. A star above. (L)

195 Cornelian. ow2. $6 \times 12 \times 9$.
A dog crouching. (L)

196 Cornelian. Scarab. ow3. $5 \times 10 \times 7$.
A dog running. (L)

197 Cornelian. Scarab. ow3. High plain plinth. $7 \times 11 \times 9$.
A quadruped with facing head. The tail and muzzle suggest a bull or dog.
Style and subject as *London* no. 872, pl. 13 (*ES* no. 1455: as a horse, but the head and neck are too heavy).

198 Jasper, black. Scarab. ow3. $5 \times 12 \times 8$.
A grazing horse. (L)

199 Cornelian. Scarab. ow2. $7 \times 12 \times 9$.
Two quadrupeds (bulls ?). (L)

200 Cornelian. Scarab. ow3. $7 \times 17 \times 13$.
Three harnessed horses. A branch below the complete animal. (L)

201 Cornelian. Scarab. ow3. $8 \times 17 \times 12$.
Three harnessed horses, one restive. (L)

202 Cornelian. Scarab. ow4. $5 \times 12 \times 8$.
Three horses, frontal. (L)

203 Cornelian. Scarab. ow3. $6 \times 11 \times 8$.
A bird displayed, legs spread, head turned. (L)

204 Cornelian. Scarab. ow2. High plain plinth. $4.5 \times 8 \times 6$.
Two dog's heads and necks attached to a single body, with spread hind legs. (L)

(I am indebted to Mr Briggs Buchanan for comment on the cylinders.)

205 Haematite. Cylinder seal. L.24.

Two registers divided by cables. 1: two recumbent goats with heads turned back to a tree between them, composed of a palmette and five circle and dot fruits; beyond each of them a recumbent lion with a rosette over the back of the one on the left, and behind this creature a recumbent stag, its head lowered, with a hand above it. 2: on their sides two men standing with hands raised, wearing conical caps. Before their heads a rosette, before the legs of one a hand, of the other a 'ball and staff'. Between them, upright, two lions poised over a recumbent kid (?) with head turned back.

Dots are drilled, circles cut with compasses, probably not a tubular drill. For the style cf. L. Delaporte, *Cylindres . . . Bibl. Nat.* pl. 31.468.

Early Old Syrian, *c.* 1800 BC.

206 Haematite. Cylinder seal. L.14.

The central figure is a man wearing horned hat, pigtail and loin cloth, holding a mace and an axe. Behind him a hare, upright in the field, before him a human head. Facing him a male with short hair, wearing a loin cloth and holding a sceptre with crescent top, with his other hand raised. Behind him a woman with long hair and long dress, with one hand raised. Beside them a recumbent lion over a cable over a recumbent hare.

Mature Old Syrian, eighteenth century BC.

207 Haematite. Cylinder seal. L.22.

Two men wearing busby hats and long tunics, open to show patterned loin cloths, stand at either side of an upright standard with broad shaft and spear-like finial. Beside them a goat's head, seated lion and striding sphinx, over a cable, over a seated hare with head turned back, a striding lion and a kid's (?) head.

Old Syrian, *c.* 1700 BC.

208 Haematite. Cylinder seal. L.13.

Three registers. 1: six male heads with short hair and a bird with raised wing. 2: a winged lion, a winged (?; unfeathered; cf. the birds) hare (?), two lions, a goat. 3: five birds with raised wings.

For the composition and subjects cf. A. Moortgat, *Vorderasiatische Rollsiegel* pl. 63.532.

Early Old Syrian, *c.* 1800 BC.

209 Haematite. Scaraboid, nearly circular. 8 × 12 × 11. Set in a gold collar (H.6) composed of beaded and twisted wire on gold sheet, and with a recurved gold wire handle (H. of whole 17).

A galloping horseman, over a bird.

Compare the early seventh-century gold mount of an Assyrian scaraboid from Nimrud, *Iraq* xxxiv (1971) 103, pl. 32.

Syrian, eighth-seventh century BC.

210 Serpentine, black. Head seal. Negro head on the back. 10 × 16 × 12.

A man before a horse. A bird above it, a tree behind, a scorpion (?) below. Line border

See *AGGems* 161f.; *GGFR* 402 for this class.

Cypriot, seventh-sixth century BC.

211 Serpentine, black. Lion seal. The back is a lion with open jaws and square muzzle, cut in the round. 16 × 17 × 12.

A chariot, carrying two men, galloping over a man. Above, a branch.

Syrian or Cypriot, seventh-sixth century BC.

212 Serpentine, mottled green. Scaraboid.

A bird at either side of a tree with a stylised winged disc above and ankh signs to either side. Line border.

Of the Lyre Player Group, probably of Cilician origin and made in the second half of the eighth century BC, to judge from finds in Greek tombs on Ischia. On this group see G. Buchner and J. Boardman in *JdI* lxxxi (1966) 1ff. and *GGFR* 399. See the next, and other examples in this collection show a floral, as *JdI* lxxxi, nos. 34, 35, 87 (red serpentine scaraboid) and two birds (pale buff serpentine scaraboid); and a lion with a bird on its back, attacking a stag.

213 Serpentine, pale green. Scaraboid with splaying walls. 6 × 11 × 8.

Three birds, a hatched leaf above. The v and dot at the side may be a summary winged disc. Line border.

See the last.

214 Jasper, black. Scaraboid. 6 × 17 × 11. Once Southesk Collection.

Southesk i, pl. 17, O28.

A kneeling bull with tail swinging. Crescent and disc above. (H)

Syro-Phoenician, sixth century BC.

215 Lapis lazuli figure of Bes. H. 21. The figure is broken below the shoulders. There is a shallow round 'crown', small horns on the furrowed brow, a heavy beard and moustaches, and heavy black hair (not marked). Once Hirsch Collection.

Dyn. XXVI or Persian period in Egypt, probably.

NOTE ON PAGE 80

Some basic references to illustrations of the whole stones are given.

A Boston 27.677. *AGGems* no. 246, pl. 16; *GGFR* pl. 355. Signed by Epimenes.

B New York. *AGGems* no. 248, pl. 16; *GGFR* pl. 357. Attributed to Epimenes.

C Boston 21.1194. *AGGems* no. 247, pl. 16; *GGFR* pl. 356. Attributed to Epimenes.

D Private. Our *121*. Attributed to Epimenes.

E Boston 21.1195. *AGGems* no. 261, pl. 18.

F Berlin F159. *AGGems* no. 249, pl. 16; *GGFR* pl. 358; *Berlin* no. 88, pl. 23. By the Semon Master.

G New York. *AGGems* no. 250, pl. 16; *GGFR* pl. 359. Attributed to the Semon Master.

H Boston 23.578. *AGGems* no. 252, pl. 16; *GGFR* pl. 361. Attributed to the Semon Master.

J London 1933.10–15.1. *AGGems* no. 251, pl. 16; *GGFR* pl. 362. Attributed to the Semon Master.

K Boston 27.674. *AGGems* no. 254, pl. 17; *GGFR* pl. 366. Attributed to the Semon Master.

L London, Walters no. 498. *AGGems* no. 253, pl. 17; *GGFR* pl. 364. Attributed to the Semon Master.

M Berlin F177. *AGGems* no. 263, pl. 18; *GGFR* pl. 368; *Berlin* no. 81, pl. 22.

N Once Oxford 1892.1484. *AGGems* no. 259, pl. 17; *GGFR* pl. 403. By the Master of the Oxford Athlete.

O Private. *Münzen und Medaillen, Sonderliste K* no. 111 (*GGFR* 403, but not by the Master of the Oxford Athlete).

P Berlin 11863,66. *AGGems* no. 335, pl. 24; *GGFR* pl. 375; *Berlin* no. 91, pl. 24 (taken to be by a pupil of Epimenes).

On the Semon Master see *AGGems* 94–6 (Miss Vollenweider made the first attributions, including our G and K) and Erika Zwierlein in *Berlin* 52.

LIST OF FIGURES

Fig. 1 Athens, National Museum. Bronze mirror from Eretria. After *Arch. Ephemeris* 1893, pl. 15. See on *36* and *78*.

Fig. 2 Silver coin of Himera. Obverse – youth dismounting. About 470–450 BC. Kraay-Hirmer, fig. 66. See on *34*.

Fig. 3 Silver coin of Kamarina. Reverse – nymph on swan. About 410 BC. Kraay-Hirmer, fig. 151. See on *36*.

Fig. 4 Silver coin of Terina. Reverse – winged nymph. About 420–400 BC. Kraay-Hirmer, fig. 277. See on *75*.

Fig. 5 Six bone bird-fibulae on iron pins. Lengths – 28, 28, 29, 31 and the two tailless 23 and 22. The eyes are hollowed for inlay. Found with our *32*, *33*, said to be from a single find in Asia Minor (see on *32* for other finds).
These are of a little recognised Classical type, represented both in the Aegean world and in the west. Our birds appear as the young perched on the wings of their mother on a larger bone fibula from Knossos (N. Coldstream, *Knossos, Sanctuary of Demeter* (1973) 169, no. 304, pl. 98) and an example of the large bird alone was found on Naxos (*AA* 1940, 284, fig. 86). The Knossos example is from a classical deposit but taken for Archaic (the Archaic bone bird-fibulae from Ephesus and Sparta are in a different style), and the Naxos find has no context. Bone fibulae from Classical (not more closely datable) graves at Locri in South Italy include birds like ours, a cicada, lion and dolphin (*NSc* 1913, 7 fig. 6 (gr. 564); 37 (gr. 849); 40 fig. 51 (gr. 866); and 1917, 139 fig. 46 (gr. 1621): C. Blinkenberg, *Les fibules grecques* 279f., XVI. 1. b–c for some of them, as Archaic).

Fig. 6 *London* no. 465. Agate scarab. A satyr. *GGFR* pl. 301. See on *1*.

Fig. 7 Boston. Agate sliced barrel from Tarentum. A lioness. *GGFR* pl. 520. See on *33*.

Fig. 8 Bern, Merz Collection. Chalcedony scaraboid. A pigeon. Illustrated by kind permission of the owner. See on *40*.

Fig. 9 Boston. Cornelian scaraboid. Statue of Athena. *GGFR* pl. 599. See on *35*, *39*.

Fig. 10 Tarentum. Gold ring. A seated woman with a bird. *GGFR* pl. 759. See on *74*.

Fig. 11 *LondonR* no. 1025. Silver ring. Lion, boar, lion, rat. After *LondonR* pl. 26. See on *61*.

Fig. 12 Philadelphia CBS 5117. Pyramidal seal. A monster (horned winged lion, man-goat, boar, bird's tail). *Iran* viii (1970) pl. 1, no. 8. See on *84*.

Fig. 13 Leningrad. Conoid seal. A winged lion holding a boar. *Iran* viii (1970) 35, fig. 12, no. 161. See on *84*.

Fig. 14 Marburg, Wiegandt Collection. Greyish-white chalcedony. An eagle and a deer. Illustrated by kind permission of the owner. See on *90*.

Fig. 15 Boston. Cornelian pseudo-scarab. Herakles and Nereus? *GGFR* pl. 408. See on *121*.

Fig. 16 *London* no. 428. Green jasper scarab from Tharros. Two heads, a mask, boar's forepart and bird. *GGFR* pl. 417. See on *84*.

Fig. 17 Leningrad 667. Agate scarab. Athena. See on *121* (notes).

Fig. 18 *London* no. 618. Cornelian scarab. Tantalos? *ES* pl. 29, no. 137. See on *129*.

Fig. 19 *London* no. 727. Cornelian scarab. Daidalos. *ES* pl. 36, no. 184. See on *146*.

Fig. 20 London E 695. Red figure squat lekythos from Basilicata. Oriental procession. H. Metzger, *Les Representations dans la céramique attique* (1951) 148ff., no. 79, pl. 19. See on *88*.

GENERAL INDEX

Catalogue numbers are italicised

A globolo, Etruscan, 40, 43–5; Greco-Persian, 107–9
Achilles, 38, 41; *121*
Acrobat, 45; *193*
Ajax, 44, 106; *170* (suicide)
Alcibiades, 19, 92
Alexander, 30, 33–4
Amphora, *60*
Anakles, 94
Antelope, *89*
Aphrodite, 14–15, 21–2, 96; *36* (rides goose)
Apollo, *37* (?)
Ariadne, 14
Arndt Group, *87*
Artemis, 15, 90; *39*
Athena, 11, 15, 43, 85, 103; *12*, *35* (statue), *144* (crowned by Eros)
Athlete, *18* (with strigil), *123* (with strigil), *158* (with discus)

Barrel gems, 15; *33*
Bear, *89*
Bee, *77*
Beetle, *60*
Berenike II, 19; *59*
Bern Group, 34; *101–3*, *106*; related to, *104–5*
Bes, 10, 35, 47; *7* (v. lion), *110* (v. griffin), *111* (v. lion), *215*
Bird, *63* (flying), *72* (two with snake), *81* (two on laver), *90* (two on stag), *203*, *208*, *212*
Boar, *27* (with lion forepart), *84* (monster) *103* (hunted)

Bronze Age, 9, 46
Bull, *45*, *47–8*, *83* (v. lion), *197*, *199*, *214*

Caere, 39
Calf, *89*, *94*, *95*
Cameo, 19
Carpenter, *146*, *190*
Carthage, 35
Centaur, *155*, *179*, *180*
Chariot, *161*, *211*
Chimaera, 16, 29, 91; *49*, *120*, *182–3*
Cilicia, 47, 112
Clay impression, *58*
Coins, 14, 22, 91, 99
Common Style, *25*, 28, *39*
Corinth, 11
Cornelian, colour, 39, 40
Cylinder, 46; *85*, *205–8*
Cyprus, 10, 35, 46
Cyrus, 30, 33

Daidalos, 43, 106; *146*
Dance, 33–4, 97
Deer, *106* (v. lion)
Diomedes, 19, 92; *53* (with Palladion)
Dionysos, *57*
Dog, *4*, *89*, *162* (with man), *195–7*, *204*
Dolphin, *154* (ridden by satyr)
Donkey, *105* (v. lion)
Dry Style, *12*, *17*, *19*
Duck, *41*

Egypt, 35, 47, 112
Elephant, 35; *104*